Bhakti Yoga Sagar

VOLUME SIX

With kind regards, ॐ and prem

Swami Niranjan

Bhakti Yoga Sagar

(Ocean of the Yoga of Devotion)

Swami Satyananda Saraswati

*Satsangs at Sri Panch Dashnam Paramahamsa Alakh Bara,
Rikhia, Deoghar, during the following Sita Kalyanam programs:
16–24 November 1998; 5–13 December 1999;
22 November to 1 December 2000*

VOLUME SIX

Yoga Publications Trust, Munger, Bihar, India

Printed by Yoga Publications Trust
    First published 2001

ISBN: 81-86336-25-7
Price: Indian rupees one hundred only

Publisher and distributor: Yoga Publications Trust, Ganga Darshan, Munger, Bihar, India.

Website: www.yogavision.net
E-mail: ypt@yogavision.net

Printed at Thomson Press (India) Limited, New Delhi, 110001

SWAMI SIVANANDA SARASWATI

Swami Sivananda was born at Patta-madai, Tamil Nadu, in 1887. After serving as a medical doctor in Malaya, he renounced his practice, went to Rishikesh and was initiated into Dash-nami sannyasa in 1924 by Swami Vishwananda Saraswati. He toured extensively throughout India, inspiring people to practise yoga and lead a divine life. He founded the Divine Life Society at Rishikesh in 1936, the Sivananda Ayurvedic Pharmacy in 1945, the Yoga Vedanta Forest Academy in 1948 and the Sivananda Eye Hospital in 1957. During his lifetime Swami Sivananda guided thousands of disciples and aspirants all over the world and authored over 200 books.

SWAMI SATYANANDA SARASWATI

Swami Satyananda was born at Almora, Uttar Pradesh, in 1923. In 1943 he met Swami Sivananda in Rishikesh and adopted the Dashnami sannyasa way of life. In 1955 he left his guru's ashram to live as a wandering mendicant and later founded the International Yoga Fellowship in 1963 and the Bihar School of Yoga in 1964. Over the next 20 years Swami Satyananda toured internation-ally and authored over 80 books. In 1987 he founded Sivananda Math, a charitable institution for aiding rural development, and the Yoga Research Foundation. In 1988 he renounced his mission, adopting kshetra sannyasa, and now lives as a paramahamsa sannyasin.

SWAMI NIRANJANANANDA SARASWATI

Swami Niranjanananda was born at Rajnandgaon, Madhya Pradesh, in 1960. At the age of four he joined the Bihar School of Yoga and was initiated into Dashnami sannyasa at the age of ten. From 1971 he travelled overseas and toured many countries for the next 11 years. In 1983 he was recalled to India and appointed President of Bihar School of Yoga. During the following 11 years he guided the development of Ganga Darshan, Sivananda Math and the Yoga Research Foundation. In 1990 he was initiated as a paramahamsa and in 1993 anointed preceptor in succession to Swami Satyananda. Bihar Yoga Bharati was founded under his direction in 1994. He has authored over 20 books and guides national and international yoga programs.

SWAMI SATYASANGANANDA SARASWATI

Swami Satyasangananda (Satsangi) was born on 24th March 1953, in Chandorenagore, West Bengal. From the age of 22 she experienced a series of inner awakenings which led her to her guru, Swami Satyananda. From 1981 she travelled ceaselessly with her guru in India and overseas and developed into a scholar with deep insight into the yogic and tantric traditions as well as modern sciences and philosophies. She is an efficient channel for the transmission of her guru's teachings. The establishment of Sivananda Math in Rikhia is her creation and mission, and she guides all its activities there, working tirelessly to uplift the weaker and underprivileged areas. She embodies compassion with clear reason and is the foundation of her guru's vision.

Contents

Sita Kalyanam 1998

16–24 November

The pandits who are chanting during the celebration of Sita Kalyanam are using the traditional pronunciation from the Vedas. There are four Vedas: the Rig Veda, Sama Veda, Yajur Veda and Atharva Veda. For this yajna the chanting is from the 'dark' or Krishna Yajur Veda. This is the tune that the seers of the Vedas must have sung thousands and thousands of years ago, and that is why I want all of you to hear this chanting.

> *Maatri devo bhava.*
> *Pitri devo bhava*
> *Aacharya devo bhava.*
> *Atithi devo bhava*

> May your mother be respected by you.
> May your father be respected by you.
> May your teacher be respected by you.
> And may your guest be respected by you
> as you respect your God.

Swami Niranjan: We begin the program with the prayer to the Cosmic Mother. This is the theme song of Sita Kalyanam.

> *Veda bhoomi Bhaarata se maiyaa vaidika vishva banaa do.*

It means, "Oh Mother, wherever you may be and whatever form you may take, please make this world full of knowledge, make this world replete with spiritual knowledge, change it to a Vedic world."

Sri Swamiji: A few days ago a boy came to see me one evening and said, "Swamiji, you are having a celebration here and I want to sell garlands." I said, "Okay," and asked him how many and at what price. He replied, "Ten or fifteen, only two rupees each." The next day he brought fifteen or twenty garlands, which I distributed to the guests, and they looked wonderful.

3

In the evening I paid him fifty rupees and he burst into tears. When I asked him why he was crying, he said, "Swamiji, you have given my family fifty rupees." I also dissolved into tears, and said, "God, why don't you give me good ideas? Why do you only give me all kinds of funny religious ideas?" So He gave me this idea to buy all the garlands in this area for two square miles.

I have asked Swami Niranjan to tell every boy to pick fifty flowers, thread them all on a string and bring them here by twelve o'clock so that I can give a garland to everyone. That's one thousand garlands for one thousand people. This is not to welcome you, nor is it to give you my good wishes. I am being very frank. I want to give these boys two rupees a garland so that their kitchen smells of food, so that these children can sleep well.

Every day I give away one or two thousand garlands. What do I have to do with this giving and taking of garlands? Do I become great by offering these garlands? If you offer me a big garland will I become great? No. One garland costs six rupees and one poor man earns six rupees each time you buy a garland. Buy one thousand garlands and give him six thousand rupees. Get the six thousand from someone. If they are thieves, we are also thieves, always taking from one another, so what difference does it make?

Yes, you are a thief, I am a thief, everyone is a thief. It is the truth. If you give a part of your pilferings to me, I will transfer it to others. People from different churches send me cash or its kind. The International Church send things. Swamis from other countries and different religions around the world send me money for many, many cows and tell me to donate them to the needy.

Compassion is the foundation of all religion; ego is the basis of all sins. There is a need for compassion in the world and for this one has to come outside the boundary of the family and add one more son to the existing three sons. If two people are unhappy in your home, you have to think that three are unhappy. One more person will have to be added because there is so much sorrow in the world.

There is pain in birth, pain in old age, pain in loss and again there is pain in the ocean of this world. Yes, there is unhappiness in the world. Lord Buddha and the Adi Shankaracharya said the same thing. Joy has to be searched for, but you can find sorrow lying on the wayside. How is happiness to be found? It is like a small grain of sugar in a ton of sand. To search for it you would have to change yourself into an ant.

Today the world is suffering and there is no one who can sacrifice his own life for the sake of *dharma*, virtue, uprightness. I don't want to sacrifice myself. I have no courage. Nobody has the courage, neither these swamis nor anyone else. We are Ravana; let Rama incarnate.

Let Rama manifest, that man who can live for dharma. Let him incarnate and along with him the beautiful Sita, the goddess, the powerful prakriti, the powerful kundalini, the powerful shakti, the powerful daughter of earth. Sita is the daughter of the earth and that is where we see the kundalini, in mooladhara chakra. The *tattwa*, or element, of mooladhara is *prithvi*, the earth element. So, nowadays I am calling the entire community to listen to the *Ramayana* because today we need Rama as a role model.

November 22, 1998

Ramacharitamanas

The *Ramacharitamanas* that I have given you deals with life, its conflicts, frustrations and disappointments. You can't call it a religious book. It is a book which deals with life in total, the life which began the day you entered your mother's womb and which will end the day you lie down in a grave or your body is cremated. This life has so many facets: mind, relationships, different affairs, beliefs, lies and deceits. There are so many things that one medicine cannot cure it.

The *Ramacharitamanas* will give you a complete idea of the timetable of life. It is a timetable of life. Just as you have

5

an aeroplane or railway timetable, so you also have a life timetable. Life is a journey and you should have a timetable.

Prasad

Today at twelve o'clock the Cosmic Mother will be worshipped according to Christian principles and, as per the tradition, bread will be given as prasad. Just as you receive prasad in temples so you will receive this prasad here. The meaning of *prasad* is happiness, whereas the meaning of *vishad* is sorrow. So this is prasad not vishad. It is given to you in the name of God, so accept what you are receiving with joy. Prasad is not of different gods. God is one and He is in your heart, in your head, in everyone's heart. That is all we have to say, and experiencing this is the aim of Sita Kalyanam.

Purity of heart

To perform this Christian worship, four people have come from Australia and one from Thailand. They are heads of big churches there. Just as we have mahamandaleshwars here, so these people are also mahamandaleshwars of their areas. I will be present at their worship too. I am an all-rounder. It doesn't make any difference to me whether I am naked or in a loincloth. Today I will wear a cross. One doesn't become a Christian by wearing a cross. One doesn't become a *brahmin*, a priest, by having a tuft of hair at the crown of the head. Wearing geru clothes doesn't make you a sadhu and wearing a sari doesn't make you a householder. A man or a woman is known by his or her deeds.

There is only one way to identify a man and that is by his conduct and thoughts. If your conduct and thoughts are sattwic, you become a brahmin, a sadhu. Otherwise, if your thoughts and deeds are tamasic and impure, you are a demon. So don't say that I have become a Christian because I am wearing a cross. If I become a Christian I will make Christians, true Christians too. But I am not going to retrace my steps. Whoever enters into a lion's den cannot return. There is no way of escape.

6

Do you remember all those saints and preachers who went out of India and had to face difficulties? I didn't face any difficulties because my heart is pure. I don't have to make anyone a Hindu, I don't have to make anyone a Muslim, I don't have to make anyone my disciple and nor do I have to cheat anyone.

Serve those who are unknown to you

Why should I cheat? Whom should I cheat? The goddess Lakshmi has given me a blank cheque. Why talk about one or two lakhs; I ask for crores, tens of millions, and she gives it to me! Lakshmi has assured me, "Satyananda, if you do as I tell you and spend this money for others, my bank is open for you. The day you use this money for your personal enjoyment, the cheque will bounce." This is absolutely true. The cheques of many preachers bounce because they spend on themselves. They eat butter, curd, milk and fruits, but I am fat from eating bread and chilli pickle.

Your primary obligation is to others, towards yourself it is secondary. First of all you have an obligation towards that person who is not related to you, who is unknown, unfamiliar, not your own. Your first debt is to him. The responsibility or the debt that you have towards your own family comes afterwards and you are already repaying this. The father is repaying the debt to his son from the previous birth. You are repaying your debt to your daughter by giving fifty or sixty thousand rupees as her marriage gift.

You might have been indebted to your son in a previous life. Now he has come to you in the form of your son. If I am telling lies you should get a reference sheet from the god of death, Yamaraj. He has a complete sheet on all of us. Now you are bearing the total responsibility for the person who was your enemy, your foe in your previous life, but for the one who is not related to you, you have no concern.

Give a sari, a pair of shoes, a rupee, a utensil, a serving spoon, an umbrella, a torch – at least you can give a television set to a poor man. What difference does it make to you?

7

Can't you think like this? You people have a path but I go straight. I have searched for the highway, the straight path, to reach God. What is that path? Never think of yourself.

Atmabhava

Why should I think about myself? Swami Niranjan will think about me. Aren't you there to take care of me? You think about me, but I will think about all of you. To think on behalf of others in the same way that we think about ourselves is the true test of Vedanta. To think, "I am Brahman, you are Brahman" – that doesn't work. You can say it just like that, but there is nothing in it. *Atmabhava* means feeling for others in the same way that you feel for yourself.

If you feel pain, why is it so? How do you feel when you are in bliss? How do you feel when you are sad? How do you feel when you are happy? Do you have the same feeling for others? No. But you do have the same feeling for your son. When a child is sick the mother also gets sick, the child's body is sick and the mother's mind becomes sick: Why? Because there is a feeling of it being one's own self. The cause of this feeling is the attachment of the mother and her infatuation with that child, because he is her own. If he were not her own child there would be no such emotion. Only a person who has similar feelings for a stranger is a true Vedantin. Only he can reach God.

The vision of God can be in a form or without a form; it can be in the form of inspiration and it can also be in the form of emotions. The vision of God can be in many forms; it is not in any one specific form. Arjuna saw Him in His four-armed form. Some have heard Him in the tune of musical instruments, some have seen Him in the form of light and others have seen Him as something else. So what if someone has seen Him in such and such a form? There is no need to search. There is no need to go to England, America, Germany or Japan to see the sun. You can see the sun here if you aren't blind, and if you can't see the sun then have your eyes corrected.

8

So God is here. He is here where you are. You are there where He is. But He can't be seen because the instrument used for seeing is blunt. Why is it blunt? Because in that instrument there is your son, your daughter, your uncle, your aunt, and so on. There is no sentiment of selfless service in that; there is the emotional attachment of selfishness. Everything is for yourself: my wife, my son, my husband, my guru, my disciple, all mine – until this whole world is for yourself. Forget about God. With such an attitude you can go to all the temples, but it will make no difference. Keep a tightly corked bottle of poison in the river Ganga herself for a thousand years and it will retain its poisonous character. It will not change into the water of the Ganga. Of course, it's a different matter if by chance the cork of the bottle comes out!

Serve, love, give, purify, meditate, realize
My guru Swami Sivananda told me to tread the following paths to obtain the vision of God. Just as one talks about the various classes in schools – Montessori, lower primary, upper primary, matric, college or university – in the spiritual path also there are six paths. The first is service, the second is love, the third is give, give, give and not take, take, take. Only give and give. This is the first preparation.

Then comes purification of the self. Once that is done you can just close your eyes and you will have the vision of God, because He is everywhere. We don't have to pull God from somewhere else. You say, your ancestors say, your gurus say, your scriptures say, they all say that God exists in every particle. There is no place where He is not present. When it is like that, where does one search for Him?

Think about what you lack. You lack only one thing and that is you have neither studied at primary level, nor passed the middle school examination, nor got through the matriculation exam. You weren't admitted straight into the Indira Gandhi Open University to get a degree, yet you claim you have passed the MSc! Nonsense. You don't know anything about the MSc.

9

It is so easy to experience God. There is one path that is so easy that there is no other path This is the path of yoga. Always crave that! "Oh God, make me a dog, make me a goat, make me a cat, make me a mole, but not a man who goes on and on accumulating and accumulating only for himself." Crave to become a human being who keeps on renouncing, who even leaves behind his loincloth, his dhoti, his sari – go on renouncing! This is real renunciation. Yes, every one of you should have that feeling of renunciation within.

Practical sannyasa

Sannyasins do not have rights over ninety percent of the property they look after. Ninety percent of the donations they receive are for the poor, hungry and lame people of the world. I am talking about sannyasins who do not have wives and children. Those of you who don't have wives and children, please send ninety percent of your wealth, ninety rupees out of a hundred, to me. To me means in my name. Each sannyasin should adopt one *panchayat,* one district, and make it green. Go to a village where even a cycle or a bullock cart can't go. Go to that place – that is your renunciation, that is your sadhana, that is your austerity.

Sannyasins should never live in municipal, modified areas because the needs of people living in such areas are artificial and unnecessary. Is there any need for a television set? Any need for a cycle? No. Those who live in villages and not in municipal areas meet people who require the basic necessities of life. The basic need is that every member of every family should have two *rotis,* two pieces of bread – this is our duty towards God.

If God doesn't perform this duty then it is the duty of a sannyasin to do it, because the position of a sannyasin is even higher than God in such a situation. Yes, it is true. If a sadhu becomes a real sadhu then he is greater than God. If your guru and God are both standing in front of you, whose feet should you touch first? You should surrender to your guru who made you realize God.

10

The guru's place is very high; sannyasins will have to contemplate that. If you do not do that, then you will extinguish yourself in ten years time in the same way that the new generations brought about the downfall of the Christian religion in Europe. You will also face the same thing if you sit idle. Where is the Christian religion in Europe? All of us from the East are sitting silently in every house. Swami Sivananda, Swami Satyananda, Swami Vivekananda, Swami Ramateertha, etc. are all there in the West. We are ruling over there. No one asks why. But if sannyasins will not fulfil the needs of society they will be annihilated. The tradition will be annihilated. This type of history has been repeated.

In India the need of society is materialism. People here need bread, clothing and a house. The need of American and European society is knowledge. They have enough money there and comfort in abundance. They sit and rest. What else is there to do? So they read the *Gita*, the *Ramayana*, and so on. After taking mantra from their guru, they chant "Rama, Rama".

Need in the villages

What is the need here? Go and look in the villages. The children do not have enough to eat. They go to sleep hungry. I have seen it, I know. Many of you also know it. Shouldn't we give it some thought? On the one hand, we say that the whole world is my soul and on the other hand, a brother, a sister, a boy, a girl is lying sick and unhappy here in her home and is not getting enough food to eat. And you people don't know this and are busy eating idli, dosa, sambar and so on.

Start thinking about others; this is the basis of all religions. Thinking about others, especially about those who are deprived, is the basis of religion. In Sanskrit, the language of the scriptures, it is called *paramartha chintan*, thinking for others. That should be part of our life, our earning, our thoughts, our power, our capability and our resources.

11

Our industries should spare a part of their profits for those sections of society whom we call the have-nots. In India the number of have-nots is not less than forty percent, rather it is more than sixty percent. In our country at least forty percent of people do not eat daily. Go and see for yourself. Forty percent of people in Indian villages don't eat every day. Can't you understand this much? Don't you have this much compassion and kindness in your heart? Don't you have this much concern in your mind? How has your prana become so hard?

We have been associated together for many lives. This relationship is not of any one birth. Today you have no family relationship with me but, who knows, you could have been my father in a previous birth. In another birth I could be your daughter, or you could be my wife, or I could be your wife. Who knows? In eighty-four lakh life cycles human beings have been meeting each other on one pretext or another. In the *Bhagavad Gita* (4:5) Lord Krishna has said to Arjuna:

> *Bahuni me vyateetani janmaani tava chaarjuna*
> *Tanyaham veda sarvani na tvam vettha Parantapa*

"O Arjuna, you and I have passed through many births, I remember them all but you do not."

* * *

Yajna of Tripura Saundhari

It is an auspicious day when, as per our Aagama Shastras, we are seeing the yajna of Tripura Saundhari, the goddess Lalita, of the Sri Yantra. It is tantric worship. We have two types of worship: *Aagama*, induction and *Nigama*, knowledge. All the tantras come under Aagama Shastra. These tantric practices are very powerful. Next year we are going to have nine days of yajna here. Yajna will be conducted day and night.

How much people enjoy this! There is no need to concentrate the mind, no need to fight with the mind, because the mind is also enjoying it. The mind that is interested in material things, let it enjoy. What difference does it make? Now the mind is engrossed in this yajna by itself. There is no need for anyone to fight with the mind; this bliss is natural.

This yajna will be conducted by lady sannyasins, but in the tantric scriptures they are called yoginis. They are from our tradition. Their guru and myself are both disciples of the same guru. They are from the south of India and I am from the north, that is the only difference. Our tradition is the same; we are one institution, not two. They have surrendered their whole life to Aagama and Nigama.

The meaning of Nigama is the Vedas: the Rig Veda, Yajur Veda, Sama Veda and Atharva Veda. The meaning of Aagama is that scripture through which we go within the depths of our soul. Now what were they doing? What were they chanting? They were chanting about mooladhara chakra, the kundalini and anahata chakra; these are very secret. In India, all of us have great faith in yajna; it is so pure and sacred.

November 23, 1998

Women in tantra

Our tantric worship was conducted according to the principles of Aagama. Nigama means Vedas. Aagama means tantra. Tantra is the esoteric tradition and Nigama is the tradition where there are rituals. This tantric tradition is esoteric, everything is happening within ourselves. They were all chanting about kundalini yoga and it is kundalini yoga that they were doing, totally, one hundred percent.

According to the tradition, the priests of Aagama are only women. The *diksha*, or tantric initiation, is supposed to be imparted only by women. But these days even men have started doing it. In India we don't object. I tell them, "Do it, who cares?" But in fact it is women who impart the tantric tradition and who conduct tantric yajnas.

13

In the Vedic tradition (you may like to use the word Hindu but I call it Vedic) women are considered to be spiritually superior to men. They are considered very superior and they have every right to perform ceremonies, to perform worship, to conduct kirtan and to deliver lectures. You must have seen Santoshi Mataji. She is 'her Holiness' as they say in the Western tradition, a mahamandaleshwar. She is respected by thousands all over the country. Women are not barred from spiritual services in Vedic dharma.

Ecology of yajna

I personally think that these yajnas should be recognized, should be accepted, should transcend the religious and geographical barriers and must become one of the most powerful means of ecological balance. It is pure ecology. You are purifying the air, you are purifying everything. In order to purify the atmosphere don't merely spray some chemicals. This smoke from the yajna is the best cleanser; the herbs, flowers and mango twigs are specially chosen. The flower they used is the lotus and the elements they used for the offerings are various things which would purify the atmosphere. So I feel that all of you who are educated and who have the capacity to speak, to communicate, must see that yajnas become a part of the effort to purify the atmosphere.

In ancient days two kinds of yajnas were performed: for purification of the planetary atmosphere and also for purification of the internal atmosphere. There is an atmosphere inside and an atmosphere outside. You know this, I don't have to prove it; everybody knows it. So you should think of yajna in the form of the science of ecology.

Future yajnas

Next year we will have nine days of yajna on the occasion of Sita Kalyanam. We will have yajnas according to the Aagama Yajna Shastras for Ganapati, for Devi. Our yoginis will also perform other forms of yajna; I am giving them advance

14

notice. Next year, for nine days you will have nothing intellectual; it is too much, this brain in overfed with ideas. Everyone says nice things, but nothing stays inside. With a broken *khopri*, a broken skull, nothing stays inside. All the knowledge of Veda, Vedanta, and so on escapes. What will stay in the mind is this nine days of yajna. Then there will be a Rajsooya Yajna.

> *Chaaha gai chintaa gai manuva beparvah*
> *Jisko kuch naheen chahiye soi shahanshaah.*

> He from whom desire is gone, worry ended,
> Whose mind is without care,
> Only he is an emperor, king of kings.

I am a king. Now if kings like me will not perform the Rajsooya Yajna, then how will these penniless people do it?

All you penniless ones sitting here, day and night say, "Bring, bring, bring. I want this, I want that and I want that too." You don't know any mantra other than your desires. "I want a son, I want a daughter also and I want money." The best thing for you is not to get even half of what you want. In one ton of sand there is one grain of sugar. Keep on jumping for it throughout life – maybe somebody will get it.

November 24, 1998

Marriage

The fire becomes the witness of the marriage and then the bride and groom walk around the fire seven times. What those seven rounds mean you will have to ask the graduates. I am an illiterate! During the first three perambulations the lady will follow the man and then he will follow her. And there will be wedding songs sung by the local ladies – *"Sita Rama, Manohara."*

Sometime in the third or fourth centuries, Alexander the Great's commander-in-chief was Saleucas. He came to

15

Patna, which was known as Patliputra then, had a war with the emperor Chandragupta and lost. Then he married his daughter Helena to Chandragupta. Today, in Bihar, seventeen centuries later, another auspicious Greek marriage is taking place here. This is a very clear message to everyone that in India we meet for union. Whether it is union with a woman or a man, whether it is union with atma or purusha or Brahman, whether it is union with yoga or even union with Rama, India is the place of union.

Sita Kalyanam 1999

5–13 December

Tantra

Shiva, or Rudra, is worshipped in tantra. Today most educated people of the East and West confuse tantric worship with tantra of the left hand and right hand paths and all kinds of other things. But this is something different, this is called Vedic tantra.

The literal and etymological meaning of *tantra* is esoteric technique. It is a technique that leads you inside, that takes you from outside into your own self. So this technique is called *Shiva Abhishek*, anointing Shiva with sixteen items: curd, milk, honey, butter, oil, water and other things, accompanied by the chanting of mantras.

Then there is the chanting from Yajur Veda called *Rudri*, which means prayer to Rudra. Shiva's original name is Rudra. *Rudra* means to cry. When you lose this external consciousness and enter into another more befitting consciousness, a beautiful consciousness, an inner consciousness, a different dimension of your consciousness, then in between you call out, you cry. It happens to many aspirants.

Ramakrishna and many others had that experience. That consciousness is a transit consciousness from the external to the internal, from the outside to the inside. In between there is a point called *sandhi*, which means the meeting place where this ends and that begins. That point of union is called sandhi. At that time a cry or shriek issues forth, and that is called Rudra. So this is called Rudri Path. *Path* means chanting. The Rudri Path is a special chant from the Yajurveda. It begins:

Aum Namo Bhagavate Rudraaya.
Aum Namaste Rudra manyava utota Ishave namah
Namaste astu dhanvane baahubhyaamuta te namah.

"Aum, I bow down to Lord Rudra. Aum, O Destroyer of sin and sorrow! Prostrations to your anger! And then to your arrow and to your bow and then to your hands."

19

You must have good fortune because today you will have the privilege of witnessing Rudra Abhishek. You will not have seen it in full before, even though you are Lord Shiva's devotees. You go to a crowded temple, pour water on Lord Shiva and after chanting *Om Namah Shivayah* have a tika mark placed on your forehead and then leave. But this worship that you are witnessing here is in accordance with our scriptures. It takes us inward from this mundane world. It takes us from *maya*, illusion, to our own Self, so enjoy it with bliss and love.

Ganapati Yajna, December 6, 1999

God's Name

You don't have to spend more time singing bhajans, but you need to do it regularly. You shouldn't do it for two hours one day and then forget about it. Follow the rules, like me. Just do it for five minutes and read a stanza or two. Even if it takes one whole year to complete the *Ramayana*, what does it matter?

We offer warm clothes to God during the winter months and light ones during the summer. I am offering you warm clothing like sweaters and socks; these are God's clothes. I am also giving you the *Ramayana* to study. Read it regularly for five or ten minutes a day. Someone might ask, "Who is that person who can be called good?" You will find the answer in this holy book.

Read it regularly, even if only for five minutes. Let us make this a rule in the same way as we have a rule for taking a bath, eating, sleeping or going to the toilet. In the same fashion we should have time for chanting God's name and for self-study. You do not have to labour too much for that. You don't have to take on a big burden in your householder life. Many people take an overdose of God's name as though this will bring great benefit. No, you need not do that. Only saints can manage such an overdose, because for that you have to change your lifestyle completely. If you also require an overdose of eight to ten hours of worship, then change your lifestyle, your eating, drinking and sleeping habits.

Sri Ganesha

I worship Ganesha, bathe him and give him food. I give him new clothes every year. Now he is wearing winter clothes. At the end of the winter I will remove them and give him summer clothes. The clothes I have taken off him I have given to some of you. Every year, if you come, I will give you more. This statue is not for any purpose; it is just an icon. Just keep it in the place where you do *pooja,* worship, or where you meditate, or where you keep your holy book, whether it is the *Bible,* the *Koran,* the *Ramayana,* the *Guru Granth Sahib* or any other book. Just keep it there. It is an icon, it is auspicious and it will remove problems.

It will remove so many problems, because often there are no problems but we feel that there are. Although there are problems, the ones we see are not the real problems. But we always feel problematic. Everything is a problem for us. So God doesn't come for that. Sometimes a child cries and cries, but the mother does nothing. Only when necessary will she say, "Hey", and take charge. So that type of problem God will definitely remove.

My father was an Arya Samaji and did not worship statues. My guru was a Vedantin. He used to say, "Aham Brahma," and there were no statues in his ashram. But my life became such that I had to worship them.

Lord Ganesha came to me and said, "Even if you do not accept me, I am your guest." When didn't I accept him? Within twenty-four hours a statue of a Madrasi Ganesh-ji, another Bengali Ganeshji and yet another Muslim Ganeshji arrived here. Now what alternative did I have but to worship them? But since I do not know pooja, I only offer *agarbatti*, an incense stick, to each of them. After that a big change occurred in my life.

God came to me as a super washing machine. Lord Ganesha came to me as a washing machine and transformed me into a sheet of cloth. Now I am clean after being washed.

21

God's Name

I have removed Ganapati's old clothes and offered him new clothes, which he has put on. What should we do with those clothes that he discarded when he disrobed? People sell rejects, but the Lord's clothes are never rejected. If you pluck even a blade of grass in the name of the Lord, then that too will be pure. If you write 'Rama' on a piece of paper, can you find the courage to put your feet on it? Your mind won't allow you to do that.

You have seen the Sikh priests holding the *Guru Granth Sahib* high above their heads as a mark of respect. That too is paper, but it is also an account of the Lord's deeds, His lila. We sing His praises from it and therefore it is sacred. Wherever the Lord's name is written becomes sacred, whether it is on paper, cloth, water, a river, a mountain, the sky, earth, ether or anything else. No sooner is the Lord's name given to it than it becomes sacred.

I have given you a statue of Ganesha and I will also be giving one to those of you who have not yet received one. I have four Ganeshas and there is a very long story behind them. I do not claim that what I am doing is correct or incorrect, but it is being done under His orders. I am not doing this on my own. So now is the time for Saraswati Yajna.

Fasting

Many people have asked about the purpose of fasting. You have to observe a fast during a yajna and other spiritual ceremonies. This is nothing new. What did the seer Vashishtha say to Ramachandraji before his coronation? He asked Rama to maintain austerity because his coronation was scheduled for the day after. This is written and you should read it.

Many of you go elsewhere for lectures on Vedanta and the *Gita*. Those lectures are different from what is taking place here. Here you have come to worship and this is a temple. That is why I washed your feet at the gate. Otherwise why would we wash your feet as you entered? We wash your feet because it is mandatory to do so before you enter a temple. This is very important.

You have come here to do pooja and not for satsang. There should be purity of body and mind during pooja. We are talking now, but suppose a noisy band starts playing tunes inside your head. Then what would happen? You would hear the band, wouldn't you? This has to stop even within your mind; there should be no distractions.

Say someone habitually smokes bidis. After some time, they get up, go outside and have a smoke. Then after some time someone else remembers tea and goes out to the tea shop. Then he eats samosas and takes a rasgulla, and after that he urinates. My dog urinates only once in twenty-four hours, but 'God's dogs' urinate every hour! Now tell me, whose kundalini will awaken, yours or the dog's? Because you should know that urination has a relationship with the prostate gland, which is closely related to mooladhara chakra.

So firstly, fasting means purity of the body. This is necessary if you are to sit for three hours of worship. The mind too should not be dissipated, that is important. There are rules like this during the yajna and during the marriage ceremony too. The second point is that you want to fill your pitcher without plugging the hole down below. This is not going to happen; you have to plug the hole first.

I am not telling you to fast completely, but those who are fasting should wait until two or three in the afternoon. Before that you should not bother to eat, because God has desired that you fast. You can take water and tea also, although tea shouldn't be necessary during these winter months as there is no fear of dehydration. In summer people take it to ward off dehydration, otherwise even water would not be necessary.

Sattwa guna

Very strong powers emanate from a yajna like this one. Mantras, as you know, are chanted during the pooja. There are Vedic yajnas and tantric yajnas. This one is tantric and it is is performed by women. According to the scriptures, males have no authority to perform tantric yajnas. Tantric anushthana is always performed by women. The Shiva abhishek performed the other day was conducted by men because it is a Vedic yajna. When tantric acts are performed a lot of power and energy emanates, and the mind should be sublime to accept that.

I was telling you that fasting is necessary for sublimity and purity. All the great saints used to do it for sattwa guna. The purpose of fasting is to increase the quantum of sattwa in the body, so that you can sit quietly during the yajna for three hours, or in pooja for an hour, without any disturbance or mental fluctuation. Otherwise, every now and then you go out for food, for a smoke, for tea, for entertainment, or for nothing. Well, this is how the mind is. It is a monkey mind. The problem is that the mind is a monkey by nature, and that you know. If you give it a little cognac then you know it becomes a super-monkey. Then a scorpion bites the monkey and it becomes a super-super-monkey! Our mind is that monkey.

Become nice

Yoga is doing one thing at one time for a given period of time. But for that the body should also cooperate. So when you are in an anushthana you have to fast. This is the rule, although it is not compulsory. We have arranged the programs in such a way that you not only feel nice, you not only feel good, you become nice, you become good. My purpose is not to create an impression that everything here is nice. My purpose is to create auspiciousness, to create an energy field, a spiritual aura, a spiritual field like you get in a church, or a temple, or a holy place. That is the point – this place is like a temple and that is why the swamis are washing your feet and giving you a tika initiation.

24

You have not come here for discourses, you are not in a seminar and the purpose is not entertainment. Entertainment has never been my way of life. There are many things available for entertainment. You say, "I feel nice, very nice." You feel very nice in a centrally heated room when it is cold outside. You feel nice when it is very hot outside and you are in an air conditioned room. You feel very nice in a five star hotel when you have a cosy bed. You feel very nice when you have a scotch. There are so many ways to feel nice – why come here to feel nice? You don't come here to feel good but to become good.

Your mind should become peaceful. If your son is ailing, you should know that he will be alright. If you have a business problem, it should go away. If you have any problem in your life, it should go away. The purpose behind all this is to help you get rid of your problems in life and attain peace, prosperity and good health.

Tantric yoginis

Those sannyasins who have seen yajnas in India will tell you that these yoginis from South India are the best, their pronunciation, actions, system, and so on, but the best thing is that they belong to my tradition. They are like us but they have gone into the path of tantra, not into yoga, so they have a separate institution. It is your good fortune to be able to witness this Sudarshan Yajna today.

My simple problem is that I will not eat. I will just sit down here. When the yajna is over I will go to my room. I am not a tea addict, but if I get some I won't mind. If I don't get any, who cares? In the evening I will eat boiled vegetables. I always have vegetables steamed a little bit. So, those of you who are fasting are welcome to do so, but please make a point of sitting at the yajna for three hours before anything else. Go out and do whatever you need to, and then sit down here quietly and tune into the mantra chanting .

There was a lady saint in India, who now is no more, called Anandamai Ma. She is well known all over the West

25

and India as a realized person. She used to have gatherings like this from time to time. Her disciples and even sannyasins used to go. Sannyasins of repute like Swami Akhandananda and Swami Chidananda also used to attend her programs. She would give brahma khichari at twelve o'clock. *Brahma khichari* is dal, rice and vegetables mixed together. Once in twenty-four hours we would all eat that brahma khichari and the whole day would be spent in the serene, life-uplifting and inspiring atmosphere of divine things. So be sure you are not disturbed by your body, by your mind, by your addictions, by your good and bad habits, by your compulsions, by your reflexes or anything else.

Chanting at home

I have to say something about the readings from the *Ramacharitamanas*. We chant it every morning at four o'clock. Sometimes there are five people, sometimes only two and at times there is only one swami. Sometimes people come from Munger and then the number increases to eight or ten. There are a lot of people now.

I am telling you this for a reason. If you perform this reading in your home, there is no need to gather a crowd. If the head of the house returns from work and goes to sleep after eating dinner, those who were at home all day should do the reading. Then God will dwell in your home. Shouldn't God dwell in your house? So, to invite God and to find a place for Him in your home, you should do that chanting regularly. To have God's power in your house, how much time do you need? Even twenty minutes will do; read two stanzas only. I told you this last year and I am repeating it again.

* * *

Bihar Yoga Bharati

Bihar Yoga Bharati is our institute of the higher faculty of yoga, a university as you call it. It imparts degree courses in yoga. It is the only son of the Bihar School of Yoga. The

26

Bihar School of Yoga was a primary school, and Bihar Yoga Bharati is a university. It is like a farmer's son who becomes a district magistrate or a High Court judge. Bihar Yoga Bharati has reached out all over the world. Now we are working to integrate it with other universities in Europe and America.

Swami Niranjan: We are going to coordinate Bihar Yoga Bharati with several other universities of the world. We have informal relationships with Sydney University, Tokyo University, with McMaster University in Canada and with Texas University in Austin, USA.

Sri Swamiji: Many people come here because they find that yoga is not a religion as they had thought. When I was leaving my guru's ashram, he asked me to give yoga a distinguished place. That has been done by the Bihar School of Yoga, so I have accomplished the task given by my guru. I have given yoga a place of respect.

Today yoga teachers from Munger teach yoga in schools all over the country. They go to all the Navodaya Vidyalayas which were opened during Rajiv Gandhi's tenure and to the central schools. Yoga is even taught now in the Defence Services.

The Chief Minister of Andhra Pradesh has instructed members of the parliamentary legislative assembly, police personnel, people in the I.A.S. and other echelons of administration in that state to learn yoga. The documents to establish ways and means for that are being prepared. The state government of Andhra Pradesh is doing everything it can to teach yoga.

Yoga and the Defence Services

We have a very good relationship with our army personnel. Our sannyasins have been to Siachen, Leh, and trained the army personnel there. Did you know that the height of the Siachen glacier is twenty-five thousand feet above sea level? Breathing problems and heart trouble happen at around eighteen thousand feet. Many people experience this at Badrinath.

At twenty-five thousand feet the army personnel carry heavy guns and pack up to twenty-five kilos of other weight while climbing the hills. Because of the high altitude, they also need oxygen cylinders. My view is that the units which go to high altitudes, sixteen or eighteen thousand feet above sea level, should practise more pranayama. They should practise bhastrika and kapalbhati for about an hour. If they can do that, they will have no difficulty in performing at high altitudes.

We have also trained members of the armed forces in the desert, and we are going to have a permanent yoga unit in the Desert Deployment Centre in Rajasthan.

Yogic diet

I am speaking about yoga and not about war. Yoga has become so imperative now that you can use it in your kitchen too. If you use it in your kitchen then the cost of condiments, which are worthess, will stop. Your expenditure on *ghee,* clarified butter, will also stop, and once you stop ghee your doctor's bill will be reduced because ghee causes certain diseases, whether you agree or not.

In olden times people took ghee and didn't suffer because they walked about one and a half miles just to attend to nature's call. Now you just sit on the toilet in your house and you do not move. Previously the ghee was digested overnight, but now before one day's supply is digested another dose enters the system and subsequently the heart is affected. When you consult a physician he advises you even to stop salt, as you have developed hypertension. So think about it. You were taking ghee and now even salt has to be stopped. It is said that when you die, your wife is left behind and when you get sick, salt is left behind.

You can avoid these troubles if you stop eating these things early on. If you do that you will not be caught by the habit. I decided early that I would not eat ghee or drink milk and my cholesterol does not increase. Someone might tell you to eat green chilli to reduce your cholesterol. Chilli

28

increases the secretions from the gall bladder, and to control that increased secretion they tell you to drink milk. You have to get one disease to control the other, that is the state of affairs. So yoga can be introduced into the kitchen. We prepare boiled, steamed or baked vegetables here every day. But the cooks who work here lament that they don't eat well, because they think that if they don't get green chilli they haven't eaten.

Bhakti

Yoga can be useful in the kitchen, but I have to say that *bhakti*, devotion, is superior to yoga. Yoga says to control your mind, but bhakti doesn't say that. Bhakti says that the mind does not stop; it is like the wind. Even if there is no wind discernible, the flag of Hanumanji flies brilliantly; it never stops, it is always moving this way and that. Similarly, the mind remains awake even in dreams. Even if you die it remains awake, and the assets that you leave behind at death you get afterwards. Shankaracharya spoke about this in *Mohamudgara*, which begins, *"Bhaja Govindam, Bhaja Govindam."*

> *Punarapi jananam, punarapi maranam,*
> *Punarapi jananee jathare shayanam.*

> Birth again, death again,
> Again sleeping in the womb of the mother.

Bhakti says, "Why try to control the mind when it is not a subject of control, when it never stops, when its nature is continuous movement. God has said that it is the nature of the mind to chatter just as it is the nature of ice to be cold. Why labour to control it?" So what is to be done? He says divert your mind towards Him. Engage your mind in the subject that you love. If you love God, engage your mind in Him.

So when I arrived here in Rikhia I discarded my yoga robe from Munger. I said, "Son! You take care of yoga." I left my mind as it is and what does the mind say?

29

Udhou mana na bhaye dasa beesa
Eka hutoso gayo syaama sang, ko araadhai eesa.

"Uddhava, there are not ten or twenty minds that can be allowed to run hither and thither, there is one, and that too is centred on the Lord Krishna."

I do not have to loiter here and there now, so let me fix my mind on Him. You also come and fix your mind on the *Ramayana*.

Maha Vishnu/Lakshmi Yajna, December 9, 1999

Unseen forces

How do I define God? There are one thousand names of God: He is like this, like this, like this, like this! Out of these thousand, someone may understand. In this way there are one thousand names of Vishnu: He is immortal, He is untouched, formless, compassionate, loving. But still God is beyond any description. We define Him because that gives us energy and peace. We want to know. But God is always unknowable except for a bhakta, who makes Him knowable through love, because love is the best form of knowledge.

Yajna is the most ancient esoteric practice. This esoteric practice was prevalent in China, and it needs a lot of study. Some people call it sacrifice, but the word is yajna. It is very very deep and I hope that Swami Niranjan will explain to you sometime how, through yajna, you can attune yourself with the unseen forces in the universe.

These are all perceptible things that you see – they are manifest. But there is something unmanifest also; there is something which cannot be seen; there is something which is beyond the mind. You all know that, but how to commune, how to attune, how to unite, how to integrate, how to understand, how to experience? Yajna is one method and a very important one. I have been thinking about it for a long time, but I could not get the proper people to do it.

30

Now these yoginis have convinced me and they will be conducting the worship.

Yajna and pooja – two esoteric practices

Pooja is different from yajna. Yajna is one esoteric practice and pooja is another. It is more than just giving a service or praying. Mantras, flowers and light, all the natural forces, are employed. Yesterday herbs were used. You may have seen that they were passing around little leaf cups containing twenty-five herbs.

There is a lot already written in English literature about pooja. I think the most important books are by Sir John Woodroffe, who has written about kundalini. He was an Englishman who lived in India and became the Chief Justice of Calcutta. One day he somehow got into a mess when he was dictating a judgement and halfway through he changed his mind. Every day he went on dictating the same judgement, but halfway through he would always change his mind.

His judicial secretary told him, "Sir, there is someone doing a tantric yajna in order to influence the whole situation and that is changing your mind." Sir John said, "Oh damn fools – bluff!" You know what English people are like. But still he could not complete the judgement.

Then he went deep into the subject of tantra. He went to Nepal and travelled throughout India. He read the books, he met the gurus, acharyas and teachers. He wrote a lot and edited some of the most beautiful books available. So worship is not just religious, it is an esoteric practice.

Now we are doing the pooja to Narayana and Lakshmi. Narayana is the Lord of creation, who lives in water, and Lakshmi, his consort, is the divinity of prosperity. She gives a lot of food, a lot of clothes, a lot of money, a lot of cheese, maybe a lot of scotch. Anything – but in plenty! Prosperity, fulfilment, completeness of all that is intended for *bhoga*, for enjoyment, for a comfortable life comes from Lakshmi. When there is fullness and the totality of man's comfort, convenience and pleasure, that is Lakshmi! So this is the

31

worship for today. Please tune into it so that you may contact both of them.

May I repeat Your name throughout the day and night. Whether in the kitchen, in the toilet, in business or in love, let me not forget You.

* * *

Mahabharata

Today the Pandavani troupe are chanting the episode fom the Mahabharata about Karna. Kunti was the mother of the five sons of Pandu, known as the Pandavas. Arjuna was one of the five. Before she was given in royal marriage, she gave birth to an illegitimate son whom she abandoned at birth. That child, Karna, was found by a man who happened to be a charioteer from the same court and he brought him up. Throughout that child's career he opposed his mother's children. When this great war that we hear of in the *Mahabharata* took place, he joined the opposite party, against the party of his mother's other children.

On the fifteenth day of war Kunti was greatly worried because Karna was seen to be a very, very extraordinary warrior. She went to him and said, "You are my child whom I abandoned at birth, so you had no way of knowing this before."

Karna replied, "Yes, you may be my real mother. I accept it, but I don't care." Then Kunti said, "In this war then you will be killing your own brothers!"

Karna replied, "No, I will kill only one brother, not all five. Either he will kill me or I will kill him. In any case you will have five children alive."

Swami Niranjan: When Sri Swamiji first went to Munger, where did he stay? You have just heard the story of Karna. The site of the Ganga Darshan ashram was Karna's place of sadhana. There he used to worship the goddess, Mother Chandi. He would sacrifice his own body after worshipping the Mother, and then Mother Chandi would appear before

32

him, revive him and offer gold equal to his body weight. Karna would bring this gold to Karna Chaura and from there he would donate fifty kilograms of gold every day to the poor.

Sri Swamiji constructed Ganga Darshan in the same area and on the site of Karna Chaura itself. From there he imparted the learning of yoga. When he established the Bihar School of Yoga he lit a non-extinguishable flame and declared that this was the *yoga jyoti*, the light of yoga. He asserted that people would have healthy lives because of yoga, would derive pleasure from yoga and that yoga would bring about peace in their lives.

Sri Swamiji embraced yoga because of his concern for your welfare. And what do you do when you practise yoga? Half of you would fly away from here if I told you to do kunjal. If I asked you just to do neti, half of you would say, "That is very difficult. How can water run through the nose like that?" And you may get frightened and run away. As a matter of fact nobody likes to practise yoga, but still people practise it because it cures diseases and one acquires emotional balance and mental peace.

Yoga for the welfare of all
It was Sri Swamiji's vision. It is his nature to want to see people healthy and happy. His aim was not just to establish an ashram. He made Munger the centre of yoga for the general well-being of the people of the world. It was done for you, for your family, for society and the world.

The scene here and at Rikhia Dham is unique. The celebration is also unique in the sense that there is a charged atmosphere, which is very positive for your well-being. Sri Swamiji himself is a recluse by nature, but this occasion is for the benefit and well-being of all of us.

He lit the flame of yoga in Munger and the light of *seva*, service, here in Rikhia. This is the requirement of humanity today because every one of us is feeling helpless. Today, everyone has a wish, an inner desire, but does not know where to go to fulfil it. At such times a person decides

33

to come to a *darbar*, a place where everyone is heard. Being in the company of God is like that; anyone can come. The divine power which is invoked here through yajna, mantra and God's name has the potential to fulfil the desire of every human being. So you will surely feel good because this is happening for everyone's good.

Living life fully

This program is not entertainment; it is the highest sadhana being done in the simplest form. When sadhana is beneficent and auspicious you begin to feel happiness. There is enjoyment of life rather than rejection of life. This has been the theme of Sri Swamiji's life all along. He always said to us, "Don't run away from life. Run into life." Whatever actions he has taken were done so that life would become auspicious, and for you, to help you to gain something.

In 1963, on the 19th of January, when he established the Bihar School of Yoga in Munger, did he create a yoga institution for you to feel good in? After all, what is the purpose of yoga? Yoga is not easy. Ask someone to stand on his head for ten minutes or to do laghoo shankhaprakshalana continuously for seven days. Is it possible for anyone to do it happily, joyously, with full enthusiasm? No, yoga is a very difficult discipline.

To sit in an asana is difficult. The definition of asana is *Sthiram sukham asanam,* which means that your posture should be steady and pleasant. But to sit in one asana for some time is difficult. Yesterday Sri Swamiji was telling us how his dog Bhole could practise vajroli and moola bhanda for twenty-four hours. And God's dog – that's you – can't practise moola bhanda at all. You have to go to the toilet every hour on the hour, otherwise you feel discomfort.

Highest sadhana in the simplest form

Sri Swamiji chose yoga because it becomes beneficial for everyone who practises it. When you practise yoga, you are benefited. So Munger became the centre of yoga. The *akhanda jyoti,* the eternal lamp, was lit there and the lamp of seva and bhakti has been lit here in Rikhia. Events such as these are not for your entertainment. Rather it is the highest form of sadhana done in the simplest form, where you learn to connect yourself with the divine and with people who need you.

Therefore, remember that when you say you feel good, whatever you are receiving is nice. You are infusing yourself, your body, mind, character, attitude, consciousness and spirit with the shakti which is generated through the mantra, the yajna, through so many processes of connecting yourself to the divine, transcendental force, and also with other people. The light of seva and bhakti is lit here and you are experiencing the shakti of seva and bhakti. Therefore, you feel good.

Gita Maha Yajna, December 10, 1999

When I entered my guru's ashram, *Hari Rama Hari Krishna* was the first tune I heard. Before I even saw anyone, I heard them singing. This was the first sound, the first music and the first name I encountered before I met anyone. Then I met some other swamis and I went to the temple. Finally I met my guru, Swami Sivananda. He said, "Stay here," and I stayed there as a sannyasin. Negotiating with the very heavy traffic of life is not easy and sannyasa is very difficult. We have to negotiate the erratic traffic of life outside and the erratic life inside.

Kunti's prayer
After the Mahabharata war was over, Krishna was returning from Kurukshetra, the field of war, to Dwarika, his city. Kunti, the mother of the Pandava brothers who had won victory in this war, also happened to be Krishna's father's sister, or his paternal aunt.

As Krishna was leaving for Dwarika, she began pleading, "Krishna, don't go away."

"The war is over," replied Krishna. "Your sons have won the war. I helped them but now my commission is over. My duty is over, my obligations are finished, I am going home."

"No! No!" she said emphatically. "Now that my children have won the war it is a day of rejoicing, it is a day of happiness, and you are going? No! O Lord, give us pain so that you are always in our hearts."

Once you have pain, you remember God. When you have problems, you remember God. God is there when there is pain, God is there when there is distress, God is there when everything is loaded against you. Kunti's prayer is beautiful and this episode shows us that at any cost, whether in pain or pleasure, whether in distress or comfort, we should we never forget God. That same love, that same emotion, devotion and surrender should remain with God. Our love of God should not change according to life's situations. Our love of God should be eternal. It should be the flag of our life flying high all the time – during cyclones and during clear weather.

Swami Niranjan: Today's yajna was the Gita Maha Yajna, which is dedicated to the education, character and austerity of Lord Krishna. Tomorrow morning the Maha Rudra Yajna will be conducted. It is an ancient, pure tantric yajna and also very important, yet many Indian people have never seen it performed in its entirety according to the tantric tradition. It will be followed by the Maha Rudra Pooja. In the afternoon the people from Kuchipudi will present their spiritual dance in which divine experiences are portrayed.
Sri Swamiji: You may have seen their dance performance here four or five years ago. It is the dance of emotions, the dance of atman. Before that there will be the Saraswati dance in which the dancer salutes the goddess Saraswati and offers flowers. This special form of dance evolved in a village of South India called Kuchipudi, from which it derives its name. The Kuchipudi dance depicts the mystical and the mystic, the divine and transcendental experiences

in the form of stories, in the form of manifestations of gods and goddesses.

Remember that the programs taking place here are not for passing the time. They are not just religious programs either. I have arranged the nine days of the program with a view that people should come here and attain three things: happiness, health and wealth, and then go home. There is no other purpose.

<hr/>

Maha Rudra Yajna, December 11, 1999

Ramayana

Everyone wants happiness and wealth. Chanting of the *Ramayana* is being done here every morning and is attended by people who don't understand Hindi at all. What need is there to understand the *Ramayana*? Do you need to understand rasgulla? Do you need to understand samosa? There is simply no need to understand the *Ramayana* because it has not been written by a poet. A divine soul was invoked within the person who wrote the *Ramayana*. When any great power says something through you, when any great power writes through you, it is called mantra. When any great power makes you speak, it is called a blessing, otherwise we are all the same human beings.

Sometimes only one person chants. On other days it happens with full vigour, but we don't stop the chanting even for a single day. Whether you understand the *Ramayana* or not, whether you like it or not, whether the mind is diverted, distracted or confused, you sleep just as you used to sleep, you eat just as you used to eat, so how can you miss doing the *Ramayana*? Everything goes on as usual through pain, distraction and depression. Do you miss any of your work? No, so why miss the *Ramayana*?

You say you don't get time, so take only ten or twenty minutes. Just read one verse. In every house, one person can be given this duty. Just as it is the duty of the wife to cook the food, the duty of the man to earn and the duty of

37

the grandmother to sort the rice, similarly, the duty of reading one or two verses of the *Ramayana* should be given to one person. You will see that happiness, wealth, health and good samskaras will be maintained in every home through this practice.

Harla Jori temple

I have completed nine years of my anushthana. When I came to Rikhia I started an anushthana that was intended for a period of nine years. That ended last year in the month of October on the 11th day of the full moon of the bright fortnight of Kartik. After that I went to Baidyanath Dham to do pooja and then to Basukinath for three days, before coming here to Harla Jhori temple to offer my prayers.

The first time I came to this temple was not to offer my worship. I just came here one morning because it is the nearest place for me to walk to. But I was wonderstruck when I felt the magnetic aura of this place. Every place has energy, negative energy and positive energy. This place is called Harla Jori temple. It is very powerful and I could not resist coming here. Every day in the early morning I have been taking a trip here from the akhara, walking all alone, seeing the villagers on the road, and then I just sit down alone here.

I could have conducted this kirtan and early morning session in the akhara itself. Why have it here? Why not there where all the amenities are? Because I wanted you to inhale, to experience, to feel that energy, and you can feel it if only you attune yourself to God's name. Nothing else; no effort is necessary, you don't have to do anything, you don't even have to concentrate on the flame, you don't have to unify your mind. Just attune yourself with God's name. Sing His name and you can feel the energy.

Tantra and women

The Lalita Maha Yajna is supreme in the tantric tradition and you should consider yourself blessed to witness it. It is being conducted by female sannyasins from South India in accordance with the Aagama Shastras. According to tantric tradition, only females are entitled to perform tantric yajnas, tantric worship and tantric initiation. Men are not permitted to do that, but unfortunately many pandits nowadays do not follow the rules. If men also begin to give tantric initiation to people, there will be mistakes everywhere and nobody will be able to stop it.

Even Western scholars have done a lot of research on this Lalita Maha Yajna. Volumes have been written on it because a tantric perceives the whole universe as the dwelling place of a superior energy – what you call universal or cosmic energy. The tantric sees everything in that perspective.

May the undertaking of the Lalita Maha Yajna today bring good luck to you all. Due to your being in contact with this ritual and having its darshan, well-being and auspiciousness will enter into your home, because this is a tantric yajna. This is a very ancient yajna that was performed by the rishis and munis.

Correct rituals and great good fortune

Due to your worth or to good opportunity, today you are going to witness this yajna being performed according to all the rules of the Tantra Shastras. The first point I made is that this is a very ancient yajna. The second point was that it will be performed by women. There are classical details about the attributes needed by women in order to conduct tantric worship. All these attributes are found in our yoginis.

The third point is that it is very auspicious to perform yajna at a *chitabhoomi*, or cremation ground. According to tradition, Deoghar is the cremation ground of Sati, the consort of Shiva. So all of you should receive more goodness, prosperity and good health.

But the most important part is that a tree without a root cannot survive for very long. And a life without God also cannot survive for long. Then prosperity is fleeting, health is fleeting and happiness is also fleeting. If you want to have happiness, health and perennial prosperity, keep the roots intact.

* * *

Marriage

The girl representing Sitaji lives in Spain, but was born in India in 1963, when the Bihar School of Yoga was born. It is very unusual to hear that a Hindu girl has remained unmarried until thirty-six years of age. From the moment a girl is born in India her parents begin to plan her marriage: the money, the jewellery, the clothes, the boy and so on. She becomes an obsession for her parents. I used to go to Barcelona every now and then and I would stay with her family. They were my sponsors in Spain, in Majorca and in many other countries in the Atlantic region. Perhaps the influence of a sannyasin must work on the people who are with him.

Life is not for marriage, though marriage is necessary. Marriage is a part of life, but life has another aim – to accomplish something, either in art or in business or with money. If nothing else works, accomplish God! But in this modern age giving so much importance to a girl's marriage and so little to education seems to be very inappropriate.

This marriage will be conducted according to the ancient Vedic style which is prevalent throughout India. It is called Vedic marriage. When the couple return to the West they will also marry according to the tradition of whichever church and sect they belong to there. It is like having a little snack in a hotel and the main meal at home. There is no problem, we can have both.

40

King of your heart

You can see how interested people are in marriage, and this is wonderful. People have come from every continent. Just as kings from every country came to the marriage of Sitaji, these fair skinned foreigners come not as individuals but as representatives of their own organizations. The truth is that somebody rules the world, somebody rules the heart, and I am the ruler of hearts. I am the king – but the king of your hearts!

People from far off countries have come to see the marriage and are attending everything here with great enthusiasm. Representatives of yoga from all the states of India have also arrived, from all parts of Bihar like Bokaro and Bhagalpur and from small villages. Our Rikhia is absolutely full and so it is with great pleasure that we are celebrating this marriage.

Education and equality for women

To be rid of responsibility for the girl is not the aim of marriage. "She has left home and our duty is over" is not the idea. Girls and boys are equal parts of society and today Indian society has to reconsider whether or not we really appreciate the social value of women and men. So long as women do not stand on an equal platform with men, their country cannot stand upright.

In the 1914–1918 war hundreds of thousands of young men died. There was a second war from 1939 to 1945 and millions more died. England became devoid of young men and the girls had to come out and work as bus conductors, repair telephones, work in offices. They took their rights themselves. The government cannot give rights to anyone. To gain one's rights one has to deserve them. To ensure their daughter's rights, every mother and father has the responsibility to see that she is well educated.

Literacy is not the question. Literacy is not the aim of life, but one has to be well educated. Just as you worry about the education of a boy as soon as he is born, similarly, instead of worrying about a girl's marriage as soon as she is born, worry about her education. The day a girl is educated, she will find her own future. She herself will be able to build her future.

A girl is more responsible than a boy; this is the view of the psychologists. Scientists have said that the brain centres for *viveka buddhi*, discrimination between right and wrong, are well developed in women. A person who has this *viveka shakti,* or discriminative force, only needs to be well educated.

Sita Kalyanam 2000

22 November to 1 December

We are crooked. We are full of lust and passions and we are people who have no faith. If we have any faith at all, it is intellectual not real. If we say, "I have faith in God," it is all intellectual, because when we are confronted by reality in our life, the faith breaks. The faith breaks because we haven't connected.

So now we have to connect ourselves with the Mother, who represents creativity. I was born of my mother, not of my father, and I hope all of you were too. She represents sustenance. For nine months who fed you, your father or your mother? And even if you are a bad boy, she can't be a bad mother.

It is with this realization of truth in life that I have invited you here, not just to listen to lectures, kirtans and bhajans, though of course you will get them too. But from the 26th of November to the 1st of December, for a few hours of your life, just be in tune with the chanting of the mantras. It is not chanting sounds, it is not chanting words, it is not chanting poetry. These are mantras, and the definition of a *mantra* is a sound revealed to a seer in deep meditation. A word or a sound which is the form of God revealed to a person in deep meditation – that is mantra.

Mother understands
The mantras which will be chanted here for two hours every day are from *Durga Saptashati*. Those of you who want to participate in this Path, this chanting, will be provided with a place to sit and with a book also so you may participate. Don't say, "What if I make mistakes in pronunciation?" Don't say that, because the Mother understands your *bhavana*, your feeling. She understands. If you try to say roti but you say, "Mummy, give me loti," she understands. She understands everything, so even if you do pronounce one of the mantras wrongly, it doesn't matter.

The idea that a mantra should not be pronounced incorrectly is a different concept. It is not relevant here.

45

This is a yajna conducted on the basis of tantra. This is a yajna in which devotion, bhakti, is the prime aspect. The second aspect is the ritual, how the archana is done, how the arati is done, how the prasad is offered. We prepare the prasad for Mother and offer it to Her, and then we perform the archana, offering various types of flowers like hibiscus, lotus or roses while repeating Her name. Who is that Mother? Who is She? What is Her name? What is Her form? What does She do? Is She female, is She male, or is She neither? One thousand names of the Goddess will be chanted in which Her glories, Her lilas and Her personality are defined.

Discipline on the path

In order to heighten your awareness, it is better that you remain in your seat during that period. Do not worry about number one, number two, or even three and four. If you do need to go, do it before or after the Path. Keep yourself free just for five days; it is not for a lifetime. If a person cannot sacrifice a few hours of his life in absolute sincerity, austerity and self-discipline then there is no use in a spiritual path. A spiritual path does demand a bit of yourself; if not the whole self, at least a bit of your self.

The Path will continue for two hours. What is two hours? I think a film runs for more than two hours and you just sit there. But at exactly the time when the Path is on you feel like going out for tea, samosa or that poison you smoke. At other times you are able to sit quietly, but when the Path starts then the mind starts. So these are some hints I am giving you and I hope that you will make use of them during the program.

We will provide a few oranges, apples and bananas, or you can bring them from Deoghar. When the Path is over you can have them. That called *phalahara*, a fruit diet, but it is not compulsory. The most important thing is to regard food as an aid. Sattwic food is an aid, it helps us, but for those who can't afford or do not want to do it, it does not matter. You can make a *sankalpa*, a resolve, that "For five

46

days I will sit for the Path." You do not have to meditate, because man is essentially divine. If you make a resolve and just remain there quietly and "empty thyself" as they say, you can feel the grace of God within.

Ask the Mother

Besides this, when a yajna is performed it can be attended with certain desires in mind. In India I can tell you exactly what they do. Some people come and they desire a child. I know they will come here from my villages with the desire to have a small house, because in the last Sat Chandi Yajna, which we did in 1995, people from these villages came desiring a house and they got it. One mason who had no children came wanting a child and he got twins!

So when we talk about mother, we are not only talking about love and devotion. Love and devotion is one aspect but, after all, we can also ask her for some pocket money. We can ask her for chocolates, we can ask her for sweets. Is it wrong to ask your mother for anything? Is it a mistake even to ask your mother for something very petty? You can say, "Mummy, give me some chocolate." There is no question of pettiness in asking for something or even putting your demands before your mother. If you have family difficulties, mental or business difficulties or even sickness, just make a request: "Please help me."

I think it is easier to please mother than to please father. Father is too shrewd. Mother is also shrewd, in fact she is more intelligent than father, but then she knows shrewdness will not pay her anything. After all, what is the mother's duty? To look after the child. What is the duty of God? To look after us, that is the dharma of God.

All Your ways are different, never the same. All we can do is try to understand what You are – or we can say that we don't understand.

Teri mahima nyari nyari.
Your powers are beyond all description.

47

Bhakti is a relationship between God and the devotee. *Asakti*, attachment, is a relationship between the individual and the sense objects. We are talking here about bhakti and not about asakti.

I taught yoga for many, many years because my guru had asked me to do so. I did it out of duty to my guru's command. But if you want to realize yourself, if you want to attune yourself with higher frequencies, with higher realities, with the ultimate truth, then you have to choose the path of bhakti. Remember that the one whom you are seeking is within you. God as Mother is within you. God as Father is within you. The entire process of pooja, worship, and the entire process of chanting is going on within you.

The pandit chanting outside you is just like a dream. The mantras are within you, but the point is that you cannot remember. Just as a blind man is taken by the hand, in the same way I am also trying to lead you. And the point is not outside, the point is within you. That truth, God, the Mother or the Father or the guru whom you are searching for outside is within. Still, you should search outside because that is the way. You cannot say you should not search outside. You have to search for a guru outside, you have to search for God outside, in the church, the temple, anywhere, but ultimately – "Oh man! Where are you searching for Me? I am so close to you. I am neither in the temple nor in the mosque. I am neither in Kabaa, the holy place of the Muslims, nor in Kailash, the holy mountain of the Hindus."

If you read and study the *Devi Bhagavat Purana*, there is a chapter in which it describes in detail the land, the mansion, the palace, the home, the seat and the place of Chandi. After hearing about how many rivers, mountains, lakes and gardens there are, and there is a wealth of description, as if the distances are in millions and billions and trillions of miles, one says, "What nonsense it is talking about! There is no such place with trillions, billions and millions of miles on Earth." So everything appears to be false. But this is not the correct approach. We are talking

48

about a time and space which is spiritual, not physical. It can be millions of miles, it can be infinite.

It says, "There the Devi is surrounded by her attendant girls." You can read the *Devi Bhagavatam* yourself. I am only giving you a little hint about it. And where is that land that the *Devi Bhagavatam* talks about? Where is that place? "Verily," the Purana says, "that is in you." Shankaracharya also spoke about this in *Saundarya Lahari* (v. 9):

Maheem moolaadhaare kamapi manipoore hutavaham
Sthitam svaadhishthaane hridi marutamaakaashamupari
Mano'pi bhroomadhye sakalamapi bhittvaa kulapatham
Sahasraare padme saha rahasi patyaa viharase.

"Having penetrated the earth element of mooladhara, the elements in manipura and swadhisthana, air in the heart, space above that and mind between the eyebrows You, ascending the Kula path of sushumna, play with your consort in the solitude of sahasrara, the thousand petalled lotus."

In the lotus of sahasrara live and enjoy with your husband. That is the concept of Devi. That is the concept of Mother. And that, exactly, is what I am talking about in detail, theoretically, so that you know exactly what we are trying to do here.

Sankalpa should be secret

This year I will also join in the worship. In previous years I was only an observer, but this year I will be a participant. My resolve, because I also have made a sankalpa, is not for children, because I have enough and I don't even remember their names. Money? No, I have plenty, so much that I can't look after it and everyone else looks after it. Not name, not fame, not money, and I have very good health. At this age, I walk from here to Harla Jori temple every morning, and I do twelve rounds of surya namaskara daily. If you wish I can do it again now. I eat only once a day. So what should I ask for?

I am not saying that you should ask for the same thing as me because that would not be your desire, that would

49

not be your need. Just because I ask for *mukti*, salvation, you don't have to ask for it because you don't know exactly what mukti means. No, I will make a sankalpa, and of course I am not going to tell you what it is, because when you sow a seed it becomes invisible. Whenever you sow a seed, whether it is carrot or cauliflower, wheat, paddy or mango, even the man's seed in the woman's womb, it becomes invisible; it is not seen. So I am not going to tell you what the sankalpa will be. And if you have a sankalpa, please do not tell anyone either, even after it is fulfilled.

I am telling you little titbits of spiritual life. These are personal secrets. Do not make mistakes. Just as yogis are warned not to perform siddhis, similarly a person who is making a resolve during such an occasion should not make the mistake of making it public. "Oh, I made a resolve to have a baby and now I have two!" No. Your relationship with the Mother has to be very deep, intense, intimate. So I will make a resolve at that time. I will tell Her, "Mummy, You know everything, I am hungry, give me a little milk."

Intimate relationship with Her

After all, a mother knows her child is hungry, she knows her child wants to do number two, but still he has to ask. It does not mean she does not know – mummy knows all about it. Which mother does not know that her child is hungry or that her child wants food or wants this or that? Every mother knows, but still the child has to ask.

That is our relationship. I know that She knows everything that is in my mind. I know She knows what is in my thoughts. She is the *antaryamin*, the ruler of my heart. She is the indweller of my heart. She is the inspirer of my thoughts. She is inspiring me to think the good sattwic thoughts, the bad tamasic thoughts and the painful rajasic thoughts. She is the inspiration behind all my thoughts, but still I am a human being. I have to accept that. So I will ask Mummy, "Please, during these five days I will pay attention to your prayers. I will attend the Path, I will attend the worship and I will follow as many rules as this old man

50

can, because, after all, at the age of seventy you cannot follow everything. Please, will You fulfil me?" And I am sure She will.

What I ask for will be what I desire. So what does one desire? One desires what one's own wisdom leads one to desire. If you are a person with a small brain you will ask for small things. So there is no harm in requesting things from God; there is no harm in begging Him or Her for anything.

Finally, when you leave here, go with one idea in your mind – "I have nothing to be afraid of in life. Nothing!" Disease, distress and difficulties – Mummy will look after everything. She will look after all my difficulties, whether they are physical, mental or spiritual. We are human beings, weak by nature, weak in mind. We may be rich, we may be educated, we may be very famous people, sportspersons or people of personal excellence, but after all we are human beings. We have our own human frailty within us. Put everything before Her during these five days and I will come again tomorrow to tell you about bhakti.

Five day program

So for five days come here joyfully. From tomorrow the program officially begins. Swami Punyanandaji, the head of our akhara, the Niranjani Akhara, to which our sannyasins belong, is here for three days and we will have discourses on the *Ramayana* by Smt Krishna Mishra from Bhagalpur. On the last day, the 1st of December, in the morning we will feed and revere the young virgins from this area, from visiting groups and one *devi kanya* who has come from the West, from Ireland, will also join us.

In India usually the marriage takes place when the girl is fifteen or sixteen years old at the most, but the ultimate departure for her husband's home takes place at the age of eighteen or nineteen. We call that the *dwiragaman,* second arrival. The first arrival at the husband's home is when she is married and the second arrival is when she comes to stay for good. One or two hundred girls, who have come to this county on their dwiragaman, will come here this afternoon.

51

On behalf of you I will present them with a Good Luck kit containing clothes, jewellery and other items. It is a very sound gift, not just eye wash. I don't think sannyasins can give such a sound gift, only kings can do that. Each kit is worth thirty or fifty thousand rupees and we are giving over one hundred of them. Last year five hundred kits were given.

The marriage will take place here on the fifth day of the bright fortnight of the month called Marga Sheersha. This year, during the marriage, Rama will be represented by a Bengali boy and Sita will be represented by a girl from Kerala. After that with new blessings of God, you may go back to your own den.

Religion in the light of one's self

We have no problems with religions. At least I have no problems with religions because I can see them in the light of my own self. We will have a mass here conducted by Father Vissarion of the Greek Orthodox Church. Sometimes we have Protestant services, sometimes we have Catholic services. This time we will have Greek Orthodox mass. We will sing songs together and have holy communion.

You should remember that politics has taken us away from other religions and has created distances. The distances which have been created between religions are not because of religion, they are because of politics. So we will celebrate Christmas here on the 25th of December. People from Italy and Greece will make all the arrangements. The holy wine has also been brought from there. Everything will be done as it is in Italy or Greece.

We have two Christmases here, not one. We celebrate one on the 25th of December, then we celebrate another in the month of August. We do not call it Christmas, we call it Jhulan when we celebrate the birth of Krishna. Baby Krishna is put on the swing and then:

> *Kadamba ki daari, Jhoole Banavaari,*
> *Jhoole Banavaari, Jhulaave Raadha Raani.*

"On a branch of a kadamba tree Lord Krishna is enjoying the swing swung by Radha."

Thousands and thousands of girls and men from the villages come. They just swing the swing once or twice. This year it rained almost nonstop and we thought, "Perhaps now the Orissan floods are coming." So that is Jhulan, when we celebrate the birth of Krishna.

But then it becomes very confusing. Am I performing Christ-mas or Krishna-mas? After all, the only difference between them is 't' and 'n'. So we celebrate Krishna-mas during Jhulan for five days during August. I do not invite outsiders at that time; it is meant only for the people of Deoghar and the ashram centres. We have beautiful decorations, all from nature: one day banana decorations, then flower decorations, then grass decorations, and so on. Krishna himself is also decorated very well and he always enjoys his swing.

* * *

Connection between South and North India

I have not spoken Tamil for the last thirty years, but I know all the Tamil literature and I can speak in Tamil for hours. I am a very good Tamil speaker though I am not Tamilian, I am a North Indian from Kumaon. But I like Tamil very much because if you put a little pebble in a tinbox and shake it, khad-khad, khad-khad – Tamil!

This is the one language which, funnily enough, has no hard consonants. Dravidian languages have no hard consonants. If they have to write the word Govinda, they can't, they will write Kopinda. They can't write Bhagavan because there is no 'bha', so they will say 'bawan'. They could not write Sanskrit in their language so they invented another script, or *lipi*, called *granthi lipi*, in order to write Sanskrit. All the Sanskrit Shastras are written in granthi lipi and have 'ka', 'kha', 'ga', 'gha' syllables which aren't present in the original Dravid lipi. Japan has the same problem. It has two lipis: Japanese and one created for Sanskrit texts.

53

But the Tamil language is wonderful and the people are too. I am talking of the time from 1940 to 1945, when I visited South India. In the villages men wore just a loincloth. A farmer would plough his fields wearing only a loincloth and a cloth wrapped around his head. The poverty was such that they couldn't afford to wear shoes. Now they are progressing very well, but earlier there was too much poverty in South India. They used to eat *padaid*, or stale rice. You put water in the leftover cooked rice in the evening and eat it in the morning. The question of cereals or vegetables did not arise. But over a few years these people have advanced and become well educated.

There are vast temples in South India. Look at the temples of Rameshwaram, Madurai and Srishailam in South India. That temple is as good as a city or a town. Such big temples do not exist in North India. In North India there are only small temples as most of the big temples were destroyed. Despite everything, however, a person seeking sannyasa has to come to North India for the pilgrimage of four *dhams*, or holy places.

Peace

I want to give you a few ideas, very simple ones, not just religious ones. These ideas are very intimately related to our daily life. Everyone, whether they are Hindus, Christians or Muslims, whether they are rich or poor, men or women – their peace of mind has been highjacked. Everyone's peace of mind has been highjacked. We feel disturbed. Don't we? Where is *shanti*, peace? Where is she? Who will tell us? Where has she gone? Where has our peace of mind gone? What is this peace? Is she a damsel? Is she an idea? Is she an experience? How did you find peace of mind? How do you define peace of mind?

When we say *Aum shantih, shantih, shantih* three times, it is for peace of the total mind: the conscious mind, the subconscious mind and the mind which you do not know, the unconscious mind. Peace in the conscious mind means peace upon earth; peace in the subconscious mind means peace in the skies or under the earth; then there is peace in heaven and peace everywhere.

I am talking about the peace "that passeth all understanding." I am not talking about that peace of mind where you delude yourself by taking a few tranquillizers. I am not talking about that peace which gives you a good sleep. I am talking about that peace which is called *Aum shantih, shantih, shantih* – and that peace has been highjacked and we do not know where she is.

Everyone is searching – the individual soul, you and me as individuals – we are all searching for peace. Where has the shanti gone? Far far away, that is the answer. But where is that far far away? Has the shanti gone to England? Who has kidnapped her? Has she gone to China, far far away? Or has she gone to the Netherlands?

This is the problem that these people have been singing about during the chanting from the *Ramacharitamanas*. Many of you would not have understood what they were singing about. Well, they were singing about this. A monkey is taking a flight to find out where peace has been hidden, where she is lying captive surrounded by the ten senses, the *dasha indriyani.*

Shanti has been kidnapped by you because you have become the slave of tensions, you have become a slave of the ten senses. This ten-headed monster known as the indriyas lives in a palace. Ten headed Ravana lives in a city, or a citadel which is golden, not stone. And whose is that citadel? Your body is the *puri*, the city, where peace of mind has been held in captivity. So it means that you have to search for peace within your self. Therefore, the first truth is that you have highjacked peace. Secondly, that peace has to be sought within yourself, not outside. This is the sum and substance of what these people have been singing about so gladly.

We read the *Ramayana* with a lot of pleasure, it is very enjoyable, blissful. But, just like Veerapan kidnapped Rajkumar, in a similar manner a ten-headed demon kidnapped Sita, the symbol of supreme peace. She is Maha Devi.

55

Duyah Shantih Antariksham Shantih
Prithivee Shantih Aapah Shantih
Oshadhayah Shantih Vanaspathayah Shantih
Vishvedevah Shantih Brahma Shantih
Sarvam Shantih Shantireva Shantih
Saa Maa Shantiredhi

Peace in heaven, peace in space
Peace on earth, peace in the waters
Peace to the herbs, peace to the trees
Peace to the universal God, peace to the Creator
Peace to the whole, peace, only peace
Peace will grant me peace.

We hear these mantras, then repeat *Aum shantih, shantih, shantih*. Because everyone wants peace, and this peace itself is Sita who has been kidnapped by our ten senses and kept as a prisoner in this golden Lanka. Neither has your peace gone somewhere within you, nor has someone else disturbed your peace. You alone have disturbed it. You yourself are responsible for that. Our peace has vanished because we have become the slave of these ten senses.

Abandon impractical traditions

You must stop this business of touching my feet. Firstly, it is an impractical tradition. Secondly, I am a Paramahamsa, I am not a sannyasin. I have bade goodbye to sannyasa, so you will gain nothing by touching my feet. Say *Namo Narayana* from a distance and just bow your head. Even if you do not bow your head, it will work.

Many of my swamis here will be very happy if you touch their feet. Their chests will expand to fifty-six inches. They need to be garlanded too and if you give them donations they will be very pleased. But that does not apply to me. I do not require all this. I am not one of those takers, I am one of the givers.

Swami Niranjan: From today the program of Sita Kalyanam, which includes the Sat Chandi Maha Yajna, has commenced. This is an anushthana. It is not satsang and discourses but a religious anushthana or performance. Sri Swamiji is himself participating in this *Devi Aradhana*, worship of the Goddess.

There are some rules for this anushthana which everyone will have to keep in mind. The first thing which Sri Swamiji has himself said is that no one should try to touch his feet. Now it is an order, an *aadesh*, therefore, all our sannyasins will ensure that nobody attempts to touch his feet. We are fortunate to see Sri Swamiji, to have darshan during this program easily and without any difficulty. That much is sufficient.

Sri Swamiji always says that when someone moves from the summer heat into a cold room, he gets a clear experience of cold; when a person moves into a hot room from the cold winter, he experiences heat. But neither hot air nor cold air is seen, it is just an experience. Similarly, you have come here to have an experience of spiritual energy, spiritual power. For this experience you have to keep your brain and heart open. Even if the brain remains shut it doesn't matter, but the heart has to be open. You have to keep your feelings, your emotions, open. Only then will your sensitivity increase so you will be able to feel the spiritual energy.

One more thing: the area or complex where you are sitting right now is to be regarded not as a venue for the program but as a divine place. The same sanctity is to be observed as you would observe in a temple or a paradise.

November 23, 2000

We remember Nasik very well because Sita was kidnapped from there. Trayambakeshwar is quite close to Nasik and it is there that my Ishta devata resides. So whenever I approach the Supreme, all my applications are channelled through Trayambakeshwar. When I had to decide about the future course of my life after leaving Munger, it was decided in

Trayambakeshwar that I should go to Deoghar, so I am here. So I know Nasik very well, not because Sita was kidnapped from there, but because quite close by I experienced a revelation.

Now the Central Government has split Bihar into two states – Bihar and Jharkhand. So you have come here from Bihar and we in Rikhia belong to Jharkhand. People from Bihar are welcome because previously I used to live in Munger, which is in Bihar. Now there is separation amongst brothers. It is good to have separation and allocation. We make our own house and you make yours. We have already established an ashram in Bihar. Now we will establish one in Jharkhand – Jharkhand Yoga Vidyalaya. If we get a good guru, we will start it. An ashram really doesn't run well just with yoga teachers.

Gopala's dance

There is a story that at one time the gopis made Lord Krishna dance. The kirtan we were just dancing to tells that story. Krishna was a small boy and the cowherd girls in Vrindavan liked him very much. In their absence he would go to their homes and steal butter and curd. He had hundreds of cows at home, but he liked stealing. So he and the cowherd boys would climb through the ventilators while the gopis were absent, eat all the butter and curd they could and spill the rest. The gopis took their complaint to his mother. She punished him too, but it achieved nothing, it was to no avail.

One day they thought, "We'll teach this guy a lesson." They called him and said, "Kanhaiya, you dance very well." "Yes, I dance very well," he replied. "Come on, dance," they said. So he started dancing, and Krishna was a dancer. Krishna had many qualities besides being the philosopher of the *Gita*. Besides being a statesman and a politician, he was also a master of music and dance, which is why he was called *bansivala*, the flute-bearer.

So he started dancing and went on dancing and dancing and dancing. The gopis thought, "We will tell this little guy

58

to dance for one or two or three hours until he faints." At that time Lord Krishna was a young boy, but even so the girls were not really the ones making him dance. But what happened? After fifteen minutes they fell into a trance and he ran away! When they came out of the trance they found there was no Kanhaiya, there was no Krishna. So that is the song we were dancing to. The only difference is that here the singer was a man, there the singers were little girls. Here the dancer was an old man, there the dancer was a very, very romantic boy. In a few years I'll be a child again just like that, and I'm ready for it. I'm not happy at all with old age.

Grace brings peace

You have a beautiful opportunity to come here on the occasion of Sat Chandi Maha Yajna. Today, tomorrow and the day after there will be kirtan and discourses, then from the 26th of November to the 1st of December the Sat Chandi Yajna has been organized here.

It has always been my tradition not to invite people for entertainment. Previously I used to invite people for yoga gatherings, but now I have left yoga behind. Now I invite people here with only one objective, and that is that grace should descend on them from the Almighty Lord, somehow or other.

Mankind can get everything in life, and he knows the ways too. But the most precious thing that mankind needs today is the Lord's grace. It is only by grace that a person can become something and achieve things. Happiness, sorrow, disease, poverty are all part of life. Grace means something different. Did Lord Rama have no suffering? Didn't Lord Krishna pass through suffering? Didn't the saints have to face suffering? They did and they accepted it. But the Lord's grace is the one thing that, if it is there, is present in every situation. Wherever there is grace in any work, in any house, in any family, then at least one thing is always there and that is happiness, peace. That is why our rishis and munis found the way to obtain grace.

59

Mother love

Many ways were devised to obtain grace, but the most powerful amongst them all was the worship of the divine Mother. Mother is always an embodiment of compassion and kindness; that is the pure image of mother love. And she is the ocean of forgiveness. Whether it is the divine Mother or my mother, wherever there is mother's energy it is always in the image of love and kindness. But the most important thing is that she is the embodiment of forgiveness. A child does a lot of naughty things. She may slap him once or twice, but her real form is forgiveness.

Similarly, we are very downtrodden people. We all are full of mischief, passion and ill will. All the weaknesses are there and we have some bad habits. The body of course is dirty. The mind too is very dirty. We speak positively but the mind is full of poison. Even then we want to be forgiven, but this pardon we can only get from the Mother. And that is why one form of God is that of Mother.

The form of God as Mother is the form that was there at the very beginning of creation. The divine Mother is the Adya Shakti. She is the Adi Janani of Brahma, Vishnu and Mahesh, and exists in the heart of all beings. This Devi Shakti is the answer to all mankind's difficulties, poverty and sickness. This is what our rishis and munis of India have told us since time immemorial and that is why there will be the Sat Chandi Yajna, which you have all come here to join.

So try to be a little more sincere and serious while participating in it. Ensure that you do not have to get up for number one and two or wander away for number three and four. From the 26th there will be pooja, worship, in the morning from eight to ten o'clock, and I will be participating in that. Then there will be recitation of the Path for two hours and it will also continue in the afternoon for another two hours.

Join in the Path, the chanting, and do it fully on each of these days. Try to control getting up in between. If you need to urinate often then drink less water, drink less tea.

If you feel sleepy then eat less. Keep a few oranges, bananas or apples in your bag.

Ask but make a promise also

I am telling you what I believe. A lot of people say that you should not ask God for anything. I say, if you don't expect anything from God, then how can you expect something from the tax collector? Yet you don't feel shy there. Why do you feel shy about asking God for something You have made this law not to ask God for anything. You won't demand anything from God, but all the wealth belongs to Him. He is the Landlord. He is the Master of all the wealth around. If you don't ask Him, then whom do you intend to ask? Man has always been demanding. If man stops asking for things, then the Lord will have no work. He will sit at His desk the whole day and scare away flies.

The reason why I am telling you all this in a joking manner is that you should not hesitate at all in asking God for something. You should not feel any guilt. But if you ask Him for something small, then you should make a small promise to Him as well. This is a secret I am telling you. Once I asked Him for a big thing, but I promised Him a big thing as well. So when you ask for something from the divine Mother, for a son, or for wealth or anything else, do not say, "I will give you two hundred and fifty grams of sweets." Give something such that even the Lord Almighty becomes happy.

So for these six days we will worship in the form of Sat Chandi Yajna. Then on the 1st of December there will be the worship of the virgin girls. For this we have invited virgin girls from our country and some have also come from overseas. They will be looked on as being the form of the Mother. They will be worshipped as Mother, as Devi, and only then will our worship be complete.

Merits from worship and restraint

At that time I will be in the pooja itself. There will be no time to meet you, which is why I am explaining everything now. While you are here in the worship, think that it is taking place in your own home. Feel as if you are the one having this worship conducted. Think and feel as if you are invoking the divine Mother's blessings and beckoning Her to descend. It is not the preacher but you who are doing the whole thing – this should be the feeling.

Feel that during this time you have earned divine merits. Practise restraint as much as possible and the result will be very rewarding. Last time there was a Sat Chandi Yajna many people did pray and ask for things and many of them got results.

This is a very important period because God is being worshipped as Mother. God as Mother, a replica of love, compassion and eternal forgiveness. Each day there will be recitation of mantras. You may not be able to read Sanskrit, but you can attune yourself with the vibrations of the mantras because the pandits who will be chanting are of a very high calibre.

Try to impose very small restrictions on yourself, if it is at all necessary. During that period stay here, don't just go out whenever you like. Nowadays we are used to just doing what we like because we say, " This life is mine. What have you got to do with it?" But you have to impose some sort of discipline on yourself. That's all I have to say on that point.

What is the role of shakti in spiritual life for the removal of avidya, ignorance, and how can we experience it in daily life without having to go through the rituals?

Shakti is inherent in all matter so it is inherent in you too. The concept of tantra is that the shakti is residing at the root of sushumna, in mooladhara chakra. The shakti is there in each and every individual. They say it is sleeping, dormant.

You can awaken that power, that shakti, through will, through your sankalpa. There are other ways too. The hatha yogis say through pranayama. Others say through mantra, others say through other items of tantra. But the easiest way to awaken the shakti within yourself is by developing the relationship of Mother and son – "I am the son and She is my Mother." Through that devotion the shakti will awaken.

At the time of the Ramacharitamanas recitation it was said that Ishwara has created this maya, but when looked at from a scientific viewpoint we cannot say Ishwara exists. Kindly explain the connection between spirituality and science and the distance between them.

This has been explained many times by many people. Sri Aurobindo has explained it and scientists have also explained it. What is God? Who will explain that? Who can explain that Ishwara exists? As far as creation is concerned, as far as action is concerned, that is created by man himself from within. The existence of Ishwara is in the atom and in the molecule.

We want to know about the sadhana that you did here and why previously you were propagating yoga but now are laying more stress on bhakti marga.

Yoga does not mean hatha yoga only. Hatha yoga, dhyana yoga, karma yoga and bhakti yoga are faculties of yoga. I teach yoga even today but not hatha yoga, rather I teach bhakti yoga. There is no difference. As far as sadhana is concerned, it is only possible by the grace of God. What sadhana can a person like me do? My childhood was spent in play, my youth in enjoyment and now the old age has come, when there is no strength or stamina in the body, then the mullah is planning to go to Lahore!

Panchagni sadhana

What sadhana will one do at this age? The age for sadhana is eight to thirty years. What sadhana will a person of seventy years do? I did whatever God inspired me to, and that inspiration came from my inner being, not from my mind. It came from my innermost being and that is why I listened to it. I heard the voice with my own ears. From inside it told me what to do, and I did that. The decision was given like

63

that. I do not believe it even today. It really is unbelievable. During the panchagni sadhana the temperature used to go up to ninety degrees centigrade. Do you know how hot that is? And how dehydration takes place at that temperature? Ask the doctors about it. I should have had a heart attack.

I did it for so many years. Panchagni is performed from the 14th of January, *Makar Sankranti*, to the 16th of July, *Karka Sankranti*. It is not done afterwards. In India it is nice to sit near the fire in January, but in May? Then and there you realize and you remember the mother's milk of your infancy. But nothing happened to my health.

This only happens by the grace of God. Why me? I had a lot of weaknesses: desire, anger, greed, ego and attachment. These are the five fires inside the subtle body which dry up the being of a person. To avoid these fires and to face these fires are two different things. I did not avoid them, I faced them and faced them well.

I faced them strongly but sometimes I felt as if I would slip. A person who can face these five inner fires, he alone can face the five external fires – the south fire, east fire, west fire, north fire and the fifth fire of the sun overhead. Otherwise a sadhaka doing panchagni sadhana commits suicide. Panchagni is a way for sannyasins to commit suicide because thereafter one really does not survive. You sit surrounded by four fires and above you is the sun. All the water in the body dries up. A heart attack will definitely take place. The best way to die is in panchagni sadhana. It really isn't necessary to get your head cut off, just do panchagni.

Shelter your neighbours
Of course God gave me a very good idea during that first year, in 1990. When I came out from the panchagni sadhana, God told me, "I have given you shelter; you too give shelter." I then told the sannyasins to increase their activities. I said, "There are people in the village who should get clothes, sick people who should get free medicine and a few boys and girls who should get help or a scholarship for education.

Also, those who are unemployed should somehow earn twenty or thirty rupees daily so that they can make both ends meet. For that, rickshaws or thelas should be given." So there is a lot of activity here now and we intend to increase the activity further.

If we do not expand the atmabhava, the sense of selfhood, then all the sadhana is useless. Atmabhava means feeling for others like you do for yourself. When your son falls sick, what happens to you? Yet when somebody else's son falls sick in your neighbourhood, you say, "Give him cortisone." That's all. You do not think beyond that. Nothing happens in the heart. Nothing happens in the head either. You go to sleep peacefully although his son is still sick. You have done your work, applied this medicine, called that doctor. You can make the phone calls, you may even take him to the doctor by ambulance, but the feeling that you get when your child is sick doesn't come. Why not? Atmabhava is not there.

What is the first thing in Vedanta? Atmabhava. "One who finds me in all beings, one who finds all in me." It is written in the first Upanishad itself, the *Ishavasya Upanishad*: "Let your suffering be my suffering, my suffering be your suffering." Now, his suffering is never my suffering; your suffering can never be my suffering.

Spiritual science – share your wealth
God gave me wisdom and that is why I am saved. I am quite well. I am very fit and fine. Every day I walk for five miles. My room is very big but I clean it myself. I do not keep a servant. I am alive and will be alive.

Sometimes I feel that I should leave this place and go to Uttarkhand in seclusion, in utter *mouna*, silence. Sometimes it comes to my mind. Maybe I will do it also because a sannyasin has to live like a sannyasin. One who can face the five internal fires of desire, anger, greed, ego and attachment, he alone can face the five external fires. But he should also have the feeling of kindness, compassion and love. Like the kings Shibi and Rantidev, he should be prepared

65

to give his blood and flesh for the welfare of others if necessary.

The hundred rupees you earn does not belong to you. You have no total right to your wealth. No, you do not have an absolute right over your wealth, you have only limited rights. I am also a partner to your wealth. And here 'I' doesn't mean Swami Satyananda, it means others. You have only partial rights over what you earn from your job, your business or from your adventures. There are others who also have a right to it. This is a spiritual science.

If you take away his right, then you are also snatching my right. You have no rights at all to ten percent of your earnings. If you earn one hundred rupees, ten rupees do not belong to you, just forget it. This applies even if I am talking to a beggar, not just to a rich man. Even for a beggar, if he earns, let us say, twenty shillings a day, it means that two shillings belong to others, not to him. That is a spiritual science, it is not a social science. I am not talking about charity, I am not talking about socialism, I am talking about a spiritual science in which you should remember that you are not alone, but a part of the whole. Aren't you a human being? You are a link in the chain of this total existence, and if you are broken then everything is broken.

In this world everyone earns for their children, for their wife, for those that they love, and the rest are excluded. But, whether poor, totally destitute or rich, no one has the total rights to his income or his life. This is spiritual science and I realized it in July 1990. Then I said to myself, "Enough of selfishness."

I tried hard for liberation but never got it. I never attained liberation and though I tried hard to see God, I never got Him. I tried a lot to liberate myself from *avidya*, ignorance, but I couldn't do it. I wanted to have a vision of God, like Moses had of a fire burning in the bush or like many other saints had, but I didn't have anything. Then I started this activity of helping my neighbours. After that I always used to hear His voice.

Bhakti

I have read the *Ramacharitmanas* so many times. If you want to know how many times, then I would have to consult my diary. I used to sit at midnight and I would finish it the next day at four in the morning. I would rest for one day then begin reading the whole book from beginning to end again, because in bhakti it is necessary to detach the mind from the world and attach it to God.

I tried to establish a connection with God, but at last I became tired and thought that with God I could have only one relationship – "You be the Master and I will be the servant. I will walk the way You make me walk. Whatever You tell me to do I will do. If You put me in hell, I am prepared to go to hell as well. If You want to send me to heaven, I am prepared to go to heaven. I am seventy-five years old, but if You tell me to marry a twenty-five year old girl I will do it fearlessly. Why? Because all is Your will, O Mother. Thy will be done, my Lord." God's will has to be accepted as your own will.

The path of bhakti is the easiest because here you operate with emotions, with faith and belief. It is not the path of pranayama, it is not the path of kundalini. It is not the path of hatha yoga, karma yoga or jnana yoga. It is the path of 'self yoga' – everything is within me. I mobilize my willpower and the God within me is awakened.

Human life is for God-realization

There is only one aim of human life. That aim is not the aim of a dog, an ass, a horse, a cat, a monkey, a crow, a leopard or a lion. That aim is only for human beings because the Lord has created human beings with one objective only, and that is God-realization.

One can see God. Whether in the form of light or sound or on the banks of Chitrakoot, one can see God. This is the most important thing in human life, the only aim of human life. Eating, drinking, house, family, marriage, service are not aims. This has to be done and that has to be done, but it is not right that man should live only for that.

67

The best way to achieve the aim of human life is to remember His name, as in kirtan. Singing naam kirtan is the first way, and the second way is helping others. Take something from your own pocket. Your bank balance will be somewhat less, but it will help reduce someone's hunger.

Ask the people of Rikhia. I came here in 1989 and since then change has taken place. People say openly that for days at a time they had no food to eat. There are people who say, "Swamiji, our daughters did not eat for two or three days." Now their daughters who have been born after I came here have a nice time.

This is what a sadhu should do. Every sadhu must do it. The growth of society should now centre around the ashrams. The number of the twenty-first century is three and this is the number of sannyasa also. In this century there will be a large number of sannyasins. Why? Because otherwise the governments will not manage. If all the sannyasins were to marry and have children, then the population would be one and a half billion within the next month. We are instrumental in controlling the population. Tell us to and we can make it two billion, and that is with the sannyasins that we have now. If we increase our numbers, then in the coming twenty years the population will be eight billion. This next century will be the century of sannyasins and ashrams. We can foresee this and you should all be ready for it.

Once we go back to our homes, how can we still our senses and mind and purify ourselves?

You don't have to do anything. Leave everything to the Scavenger – He will do it. Leave everything to God. If He inspires you to think good thoughts, think good thoughts. If He inspires you to think bad thoughts, think bad thoughts. God is the inspirer of every act. Why do you worry about it? Rather than trying to purify yourself by doing this and that, say, "God, what do You want me to do?" And do it. You leave it to Him and He will do it. Try this trick and everything will change in your life.

Khichari of religions

Father Vissarion from the Greek Orthodox tradition has
come here. We have a very good connection with these
churches. I relate well to everyone. I am like water, mix it
with soap and it mixes, or even mix it with poison and it
mixes. So, on behalf of all of us from various countries and
different states of India, I welcome Father amongst us.

On the 25th, mass will be conducted by Father
Vissarion. That will be the ceremonial inauguration of the
Devi Pooja, Mother worship, which will start from the 26th.
We have decided that this mass will be the opening of the
Sat Chandi Yajna. This is something new.

Another new thing will happen at the same time. Father
John, who until recently has been the principal of the Saint
Francis School here, is to become the head of the
Franciscans in India. The Vatican is sending their representative to conduct the installation ceremony, because it is a
very big thing. So he is the head of the Franciscans in India
and he is my good friend. He is like me, he talks too much.
You will all like him! He will also be joining the mass here,
so we will have a khichari, a a mixture, of poojas here:
Catholic pooja, Orthodox pooja and our Shakti pooja, all
three will be conducted. Khichari is easily digestible,
remember that. A khichari of religions does not cause
stomach aches, constipation or diarrhoea. It will be a happy
occasion.

All the local people and those from Deoghar, listen
carefully. A learned priest and acharya has come from
Greece. Alexander the Great's commander, Seleucas, also
came from there and when he lost the battle he gave his
daughter, Helena, in marriage to Chandragupta Maurya.
So their son, Ashoka, was half Greek and half Bihari. Now
Father Vissarion from Greece will perform a form of worship
called a mass. After that the Devi Pooja will begin. We have
included this program because the Orthodox Christians
treat Devi as God. God as Father is the belief of the whole

world. God as Mother is their belief. The capital of Greece is Athens, and Athena means Saraswati. So I thought we should worship according to their Christian religion before we perform our Devi Pooja. It will be good for us, good for Rikhia and good for the country, because our country is the only one where such a mixture of religions can take place.

Yam Shaivaasamupaasate Shiva'ti Brahmeti Vedaantino
Baudhhaah Buddha iti pramaana patavah Karteti Naiyyaayikaah
Arhanityat Jainashaasanarataah Karmeti Meemaansakaah
So'yam nah vidadhatu vaanchita phalam trailokyanatho Harih.

"Whom the Shaivites worship as Shiva, the Vedantins as Brahman, the Buddhists as Buddha, the Naiyayikas as Karta, the followers of Jainism as Arhan and the Mimamsikas as Karma, may that Hari, who is the Lord of the three worlds, bestow upon us the desired fruit."

In India we like light things. Serious things are not really liked. We don't say, "This is the only way," we say, "This too is the way." We don't say, "This is the only way and not that," we say, "This is the way, that too is the way and that other way is also the way." We know that national highway 1, national highway 2 and other highways go to Delhi, but if you want to go to Delhi from Cuttack, then you can't take national highway 2. If you want to go to Delhi from Bombay, then will need to take another national highway. In the *Shivamaheemna Stotram* it is said:

Rucheenaam vaichitryaadriju kutila naanaa patha jhushaam
Nrinaameko gamyastvamasi payasaamarnava iva.

"Persons following different paths, straight or crooked according to the difference in their temperament, reach none other than You, just as rivers enter into the ocean."

Depending upon the nature and peculiarities of people's characters, there are many straight and crooked ways. This fact is acknowledged by the people of this country. All the rishis, munis and preachers accepted this fact; it is not the doctrine of Swami Satyananda. Do not think that I am telling you something new. Our culture has this principle

70

that rivers, whether they flow from east or west or north or south, all merge in the ocean. Similarly, whichever path we take, whether tantric, Biblical, Islamic or Vedic, ultimately we reach that supreme Father, our Lord.

Swami Niranjan: The cosmic Mother will be invoked here and during this period you will have to maintain the same dignity as you would in a temple, a church, a mosque or any other place of worship. So no gossiping or jumping about in this area, except when you are being guided by Sri Swamiji, because he is the master, the controller and invoker of the forces within and without you. He can pull the strings whenever he likes, but from our side we have to be receptive and restrain our body, senses, mind and emotions.

Sri Swamiji: Now we will sing Devi's name. Devi is without name, without form so only singing, "Ma," is enough.

As I was born in the Ikshwaku family, I am a *kshatriya*, a warrior. The day I was born, my mother and father placed a picture of Sri Rama on my body and a sword in my hand. Lord Rama is my Ishta devata. My mantra is that of Lord Shankara but Rama is my Ishta. I don't need to tell you because Rama is in you also. I like Rama best. He is a good person, well meaning, well spoken and free of mischief.

All that exists is only one. There is no two in the world. In the world it is neither I nor you, neither you nor I. Hail God! Hail God. That's all. One thousand million Christians in the world accept this and take it as their mantra. Hail means, Hail Sri Rama, Hail Sri Krishna, Hail Sri Gopala, Hail Sri Devi, Hail all the gods. Lets sing, "Lord, let me see Your face in every face I see." Let me find You in everyone. Wherever I look I find You and only You.

* * *

Yajna

In the forests of South America I have seen rare sights from the pre-Columbian era. I found that the people of the pre-Columbian civilization practised yajna. Archaeological

71

excavations throughout the world investigating the Stone Age, Bronze Age and various ages have given us evidence that they performed a ceremony in which natural herbs were offered into the fire with the chanting of mantras and dance rituals. Unfortunately those traditions have become extinct throughout the world, except in India.

India has preserved this tradition of yajna for thousands of years. It has given various interpretations of yajna. What are the different forms of yajna? How does an individual perform a yajna? How does a community perform a yajna? And if at all the king or the sovereign of a country wants to perform a yajna, how does he do it? All these things have been preserved, maintained and kept alive in India even until today.

It is not only here in Rikhia that the Sat Chandi Yajna is performed. Yajna in India is not a rare event. It is a very popular event, like popular music in the West. The pandits, the acharyas, who will be coming to perform the yajna are booked years in advance. If you decide to perform a yajna, you can't do it tomorrow or the day after because there will be no acharyas available.

I am telling you this for a reason. Remember that the priests are brahmins; they are not kshatriyas, the warrior caste, or *vaishyas,* the merchant class, or *shudras*, the working class of India. Not all brahmins perform yajnas, only certain types of brahmins become the acharyas who perform yajna. Rich people, poor people and communities get together, collect some money and invite the brahmins, the priests, to perform the yajna. People in the vicinity are not invited to the yajna. There is no invitation; that is one rule here. When you perform a yajna you prepare it, then you just put posters and banners somewhere along the footpath.

Purifying the environment
People come in their thousands because yajna purifies the physical atmosphere, ecology as you call it. Yajna also purifies the *akashic* or subtle atmosphere, the atmosphere which influences your mind, but first of all it purifies that

atmosphere which influences your body. Nowadays you know a lot about the environment, about the green house effect, the heating of the earth, and so on. I don't have to tell you about that. Yajna is the cure, the remedy. First of all, lovers and devotees of the environment, all those who believe that the atmosphere should be purified, that carbon monoxide must be reduced, are the ones who must practise yajna, not only on this scale but also on an individual scale.

In the Vedas, there is a system of yajna which an individual can perform at home with his family. I come from an Arya Samaj family. My father was an Arya Samajist. Arya Samajis are reformers, just like Protestants in Christianity. Every morning, my father would position a few sticks in a copper pot and chant the *Agnihotra Vidhi Veda Mantra* for fifteen minutes:

Aum shanno devirabhistaya aapo bhavantu peetaye
Sham yorabhi sravantu nah.
Om bhooragnaye praanaaya svaaha,
Idamagnaye praanaaya – idam na mama.

Aum bhuvarvaayave apaanaaya svaaha,
Idam vaayave apaarnaya – idam na mama.

Aum svaraadityaaya vyaanaaya svaaha
idamaadityaaya vyaanaaya – idam na mama.

Aum bhoorbhuvah svaragnivaayvaadityebhyah
praanaapaanavyaanebhyah svaaha
Idamagnivaayvaadityebhyah praanaapaanavyaanebhyah –
idam na mama.

Svaahaa svaahaa svaahaa svaahaa – aahaah!

I still remember it from the time I was a small child. So an individual can perform yajna at home and purify the atmosphere. A community can perform yajna and purify the atmosphere of the community, the village or town.

More than purification of the physical atmosphere of the earth and its environment, it is now becoming more

73

important that we should purify the mental atmosphere, the psychic atmosphere, the emotional atmosphere which has become corrupt. Your mind is full of bad thoughts. It is just like a monkey which has been stung by a scorpion. Imagine what will happen to it. Then add some champagne and you can imagine what that monkey will be like. You are that monkey. All the monkeys are here!

Now how can you silence that monkey? Our ancestors, your ancestors, everyone's ancestors said, "Perform yajna." *Yajna* means offering. When you offer food to the poor and hungry, that is yajna. When you give clothes to someone who has none, that is yajna. To give and to give and to give is yajna. In Sanskrit the word yajna is a combination of three letters 'ya' 'ja' and 'na' – production, consumption and distribution. There has to be a balance between production, consumption and distribution. The *Bhagavad Gita* has also suggested various other forms of yajna and you should read it.

Mantra and revelation

In yajna there are mantras and there is fire. The mantras are those which were heard by the rishis: "In the beginning was the Word, and the Word was with God and the Word was God." That word is mantra. What comes out from God is mantra. What is revealed to you is mantra. These mantras are collected from time to time because there are many seers and rishis. *Rishi* means one who can see through, one whose consciousness can penetrate and unite with the Supreme Being. They can see and they can hear.

Hajrat Mohammed, the prophet of Islam, is one example. He worked hard in the *karavan sarai*, the roadside hotels, and after finishing his evening's work, he would go to the mountains to pray. One day he suddenly heard a sound. What he heard was the Koran. That is called revelation, that is mantra. Mohammed was illiterate and could not write a mantra, but still it came to him.

These revelations come in various other forms as well. The prophet of the Jews was Moses. He beheld a fire burning

Iranian devotees – Anandajyoti, founder of the Satyananda Yoga Centre in Iran, presents Sufi honours to Paramahamsaji, 1998

Swami Sharadanandaji performing Rudrabhishek, 1998

Celebrating Holy Communion with Reverend Antoinette Schoenmaker and Paramahamsaji, 1998

Swami Tejomayanandaji, present Acharya of the Chinmaya Mission, speaks on bhakti, 1998

Yajna to the Divine Mother, invoking divine forces, 1998

Celebrating the marriage of Sitaji and Sri Rama, 1999

Mataji from Lalita Mahila Samajam Ashram, Tamil Nadu, 1999

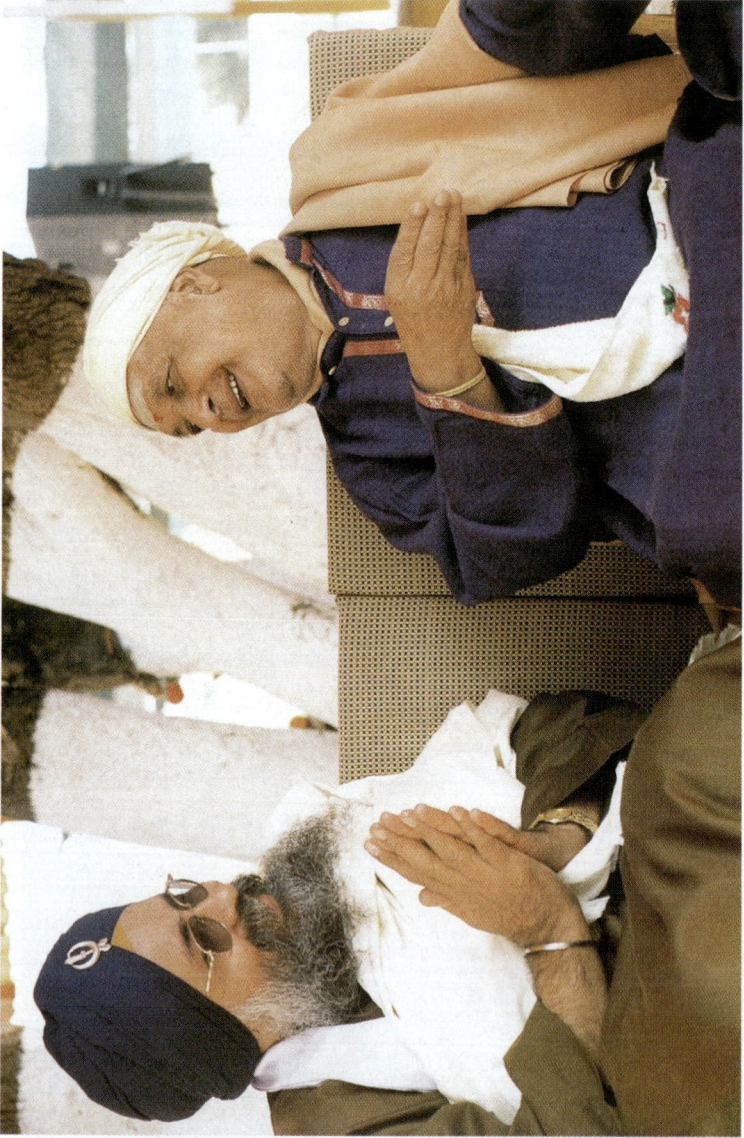

Mutual accord, 1999

Lord Shiva and Parvati competing in dance, 1999

Paramahamsaji, 2000

Greek Orthodox Mass celebrated by Father Vissarion to inaugurate the worship of God as Mother, 2000

Paramahamsaji, Swami Punyananda Giri (Acharya of Sri Niranjani Akhara) and Father Vissarion (Acharya of the Greek Orthodox Church), 2000

Swami Niranjanji with Swami Punyanandaji, 2000

Prasad distribution – give to people you don't know, 2000

Devi in her invoked form, 2000

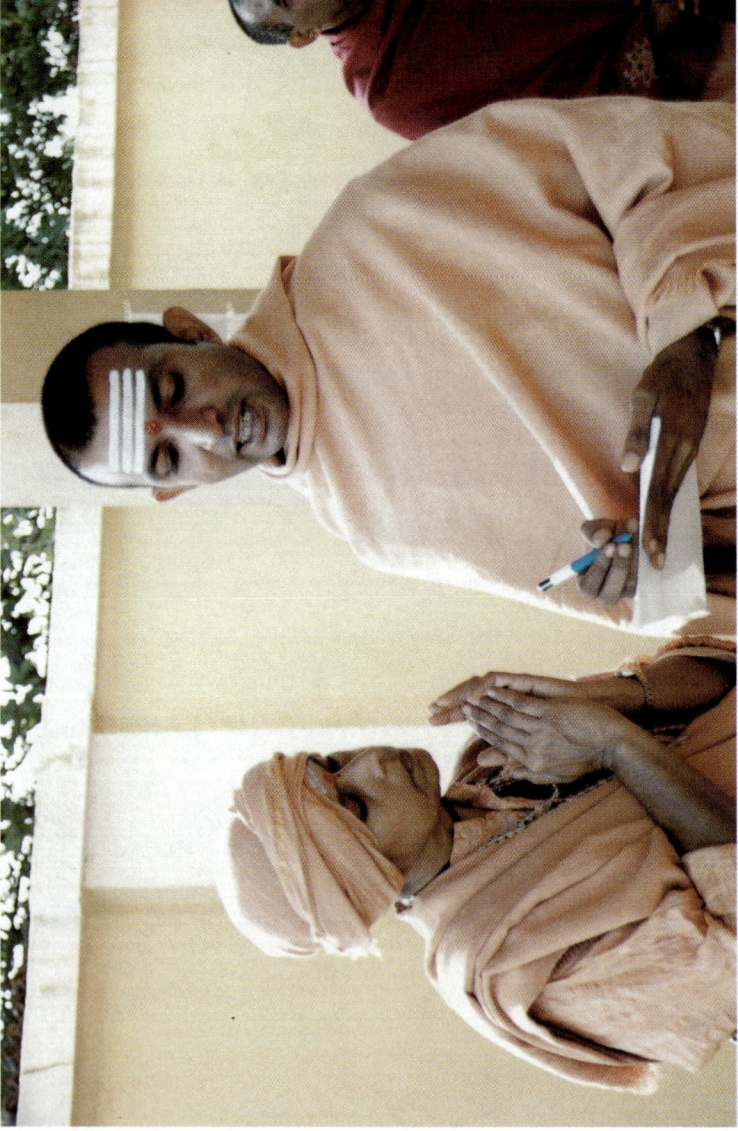

Swami Satsangi confers with Swami Niranjan, 2000

in the bush. He saw it, he did not hear it. So God can be revealed in the form of a sound. Anything can be the form of God. He can reveal Himself as a cloud. You can see Him as a cloud. When we hear Him as a sound, we call it mantra. When we see Him, we call Him a *devata*, a god. Sometimes you see Him in male form, sometimes in female form. Everyone knows the difference between a male and a female, but when we say, "Is God male or female?" we are not talking about bodies.

So when you perform yajna you are using a mantra, and these mantras are called *nada brahma*, the Supreme Being in the form of a sound. Nada brahma is the Supreme Being, Paramatma or God or Allah or Khuda or Jehovah in the form of a sound. That sound has been recorded for thousands and thousands of years in India by a particular clan called brahmins. Every morning a brahmin will sit down after taking his bath and chant a Vedic mantra:

> *Aa no bhadraah kratavo yantu vishvato'adabdhaaso apareetaasa ubhdidah.*
> *Devaa no yathaa sadamida vridhe asannapraayuvo rakshitaaro dive dive.*

"May auspicious, never-failing and elevating works, that are done without any compulsion, be achieved by us in all directions of activity. May the divinities grant us protection day after day without any obstruction in our progress."

It goes on for half an hour, one hour, two hours. There are four Vedas where these mantras have been recorded: the Rig Veda, Yajur Veda, Sama Veda and Atharva Veda. The four Vedas are not known as four books, they are known as shrutis. *Shruti* means 'heard'. The Vedas were heard. All these great books like the Vedas, the Koran, the Bible or the Torah were heard. They were not written by intellectuals like you and me. They were revealed in the depths of meditation by the deepest being of man, the God whom you call Allah. Your deepest being beyond the senses, beyond the intellect, beyond the mind, beyond the subconscious mind, beyond the unconscious mind where

75

the superconscious man is in you. That is full of luminosity, full of knowledge and full of totality. We call it God.

The battle

So in yajna these mantras are used and they are recited once, ten times, one hundred times, a thousand times, one hundred thousand times or one million times. When they are recited a hundred times, it is called *Sat* or *Shata*, as in Sat Chandi Yajna. When they are recited a thousand times, it is called Sahasra Chandi Yajna. When they are repeated hundreds of thousands of times, it is called Laksha Chandi Yajna. When they are recited millions of times, it is called Koti Chandi Yajna.

In India, the Hindus in particular have a peculiar philosophy. When they talk of spiritual life they talk about quarrels and fights, wars and battles, killings and destruction. If you read those books and see this yajna some of you will say, "What? A woman takes a missile, kills a man and then they say, 'Swaaha, swaaha' – that is a funny thing." But in all the Puranas, in all the *itihasas*, in the entire history of this country, wherever spirituality is introduced, it is defined in terms of battle, in terms of war, in terms of missiles, in terms of death, in terms of *devas*, the divine beings, and *asuras*, demons, in terms of *manavas*, human beings – you and me, the individual.

In fact, life is a battlefield and we are all fighting. The fight is continuing between the forces that are dark and those that are not. This eternal battle between the two forces continues in every individual as long as he lives and even after he dies. There is no other way to explain the situations in life except as a battle. In the *Mahabharata*, on one side you have the Pandavas and on the other side you have the Kauravas, and Krishna says, "Fight." Oh Krishna. He is a violent leader! He says that we should fight whereas Gandhi told us we should not fight. We are talking about non-violence and in the *Gita* Krishna says, *Tasmaat yudhyasva Bhaarata* – "Therefore, you should fight," at least twenty-one times.

So were these people wrong, or was Krishna a violent person? Here fighting means that you have to fight with the lower tendencies of your life, the limitations you have. You may or may not agree, but there is some block in your personality. There is certainly a block in our personalities. Why do I say this? Because the thing you are searching for is very close to you, but you don't see it. The thing you are searching for is closer than your breath, closer than your own mind. The thing you are searching for is closest to you, yet you are not able to see it. Even if you say that you have it, you say, "Yes I believe it but I can't see it." So there is a mental block. This mental block is called *ajnana, avidya,* ignorance or nescience.

The yajna will help you. In India people go with a lot of desires for children, for money, for solutions to all kinds of troubles. Some have cancer, some have heart problems, some have problems with the wife and children. Everyone has troubles, and in yajna they search for solutions and they get a solution. Your awareness is heightened. You have to make a sankalpa. Of course, if you want coca cola or a cognac, I don't know if you will get it or not. But I am not talking in these terms. You have to make the sankalpa, "God reveal yourself to me in any form you like." That's all.

What is the duty of a sevak, a servant, towards his guru? What are his commands?

This is a very general question. The people who teach us at school are also gurus. Dattatreya had twenty–four gurus. *Guru* means the person who gives you knowledge, who gives you light. Those who live with the guru should obey the instructions of the guru. Those who do not live near the guru should also obey the commands of the guru. There are many types of gurus.

Live for others who are not known to you

Do not live only for the sake of those who belong to you. Live a little for others also. You cannot totally share the happiness and sorrows of the world, this is only possible for God, but in some little way share the sorrows of others. This is loftiness of mind.

If everyone lights a candle there will be light all around. Usually we light a candle only in our own house. My husband, my wife, my children, 'we two and our two' has become our world. We have no connection with the rest of the world. With other people we have only the connection of selfishness. This should not happen. Prayers and worship have their own place, pilgrimage and sadhana has its own place, your job has its own place, serving the country has its own place. But if you want the light of God which is covered within you, the hidden light, to be uncovered, then you need to widen your heart. In the *Ishavasya Upanishad* (v. 15) it is said:

Hiranmayena paatrena satyasyaapihitam mukham
Tattvam pooshanapaavrinu satyadharmaaya drishtaye.

"The face of the truth is hidden with a golden vessel. Remove it, O Sun, so that I who am a devotee of truth may see You."

Do not turn away a beggar
You have to find a place in your heart for people who are not known to you. You have to act out your compassion and feelings on behalf of these people. Only consolation by words is not enough. "Oh see, he is full of sorrow, look what karmas he has got." That is nothing. At least give him a glass of tea. Don't turn away the beggar at your gate. Some people say, "Nowadays all these people have turned wicked." This is not right. That philosophy is only to defend your own petty mind. Think about whether what I am saying is right or wrong and apply your own reasoning. If I am not right then leave it, but nobody, however wicked he may be, will come begging at your gate to cheat you. I am telling you honestly. I have lived that life, that is why I can speak from my own experience. People used to say that I was cheating everyone. Maybe even now people are saying, "Look how much he is cheating."

78

In the whole day that beggar may go to the doors of ten houses. One beggar, even if he works for eight hours, will only go to sixteen houses. Even if he gets two rupees from each house, he will collect only thirty-two rupees. People say, "Look, nowadays everybody cheats. That beggar drinks alcohol, even saints become cheats." Even if he does drink he only drinks country liquor, he has not taken cognac. Even if he has drunk liquor, what mistake has he committed? *Soma rasa* was taken by all the rishis and munis. If soma rasa had not been available, then they would have taken country liquor if it had been available. I am not joking. Never refuse a beggar at the gate of your house. Keep puffed rice, onions, some salt. If there is no cooked food ready, then give him puffed rice on a leaf plate.

It is no good wailing, "O God, he has come to my door!" After all he is a beggar. He has a soul and that soul is in you too. The soul, the light that is inside the beggar is the same light that is in you. The electricity in one bulb is the same electricity in another bulb. It is the same electricity in Deoghar and Bombay. The same soul is in everyone, only the circuits are different. Your circuit is different from my circuit, so when I turn on the switch my light is on, not yours. The circuits are different, aren't they? What is that circuit? Ego, the circuit of individuality. If ego is effaced then if my light is on, everyone's light goes on and if my light is off then everyone else's goes off.

Two sadhanas

My second piece of advice is that in your house you should do kirtan of God's name like we do here. Naam sankirtan should be done. I am not speaking about bhajan. *Naam sankirtan* means singing the name of God. 'Hare Rama, Hare Rama' is naam sankirtan. It should be done in every home for ten to fifteen minutes daily. Practise naam sankirtan and helping others. From these two sadhanas you will receive great benefit both in this life and in the life hereafter.

According to Hindu tradition at the time of menstruation women are not supposed to attend pooja and worship. Is this rule applicable during this yajna?

Menstruation is a natural happening. It is something which nature does every month for the cleanliness of the womb. We clean our stomach every day, but the cleaning of the womb takes place when the hormones increase and not before that. That is why it is not impure, rather it is natural.

During that time the body temperature fluctuates and accordingly there is instability on the emotional front, but this has nothing to do with purity or impurity. In earlier times when women menstruated they were made to sit in a corner because there was no alternative at that time. In that condition how could she perform worship, cook or go to work? Whatever a man can do, a woman can also do, but how could she do it then? But today we have better resources. Now during menstruation women can swim, play tennis, practise asana and pranayama and sing bhajans also. They can also perform yajna. There are absolutely no restrictions.

This prejudice was given to me in my religion and I have thought about it since childhood. Of course I have matured now. I have practised scientific thinking. I have read scriptures, read the shrutis and Vedas, and I have come to the conclusion that although there is emotional instability and temperature fluctuations at the time of menstruation, as far as purity or impurity is concerned it does not matter. Certainly all activities relating to pooja and worship can be performed where heavy exercise is not involved.

Reading the Ramacharitamanas I came across a part where there is a reference to women being dull and weak. It seems women are viewed as taking men away from God. Where does this leave women in this era?

This is not correct. Woman was your mother. She was also mine. There is nothing in the *Ramacharitamanas* that can be interpreted like that. In any scripture there are different viewpoints. It depends on who is speaking, whether it is

Ravana or Rama. There cannot be one single view. The point is whether the devil or God is saying it. Sometimes there are interpolations where lines have been inserted after the text was written.

You should also consider that from time to time our society has had various views about women. It is only today that women are freer and able to speak out. There was a time when they were used as slaves. Even now they are all *naukaranis*, maidservants. That has to be corrected. But in the *Ramacharitamanas,* the author, Tulsidas, has very great respect for womankind.

November 26, 2000

Sat Chandi Yajna

Today was really blissful and many, many people joined in the chanting. Everyone was chanting with so much bliss. Tomorrow it will also be done in a similar manner. There is nothing to explain about the do's and the don'ts. When you eat a rasgulla, how can I tell you to experience the sweetness? When someone eats fried sweets or kheer, it is not necessary to tell them to experience the sweetness. You have to experience it for yourself. If your taste buds are sensitive enough, then you will enjoy the sweetness of the rasgullas.

There is only one God before whom one should bow one's head. He is the only VIP here. Don't do topsy turvy things. If a little is offered there and a little is offered here, where is your mind? You have only one mind, not ten or twenty. You also have only one heart. You have come for worship of Devi. Keep your mind and heart focused on that experience alone.

Village seva

This man, Tetu Ramani, is the *pradhan*, the chief of this village and this area. The land where the lake, the *sarovar*, has been constructed was donated by him. He said that before we came the people here did not eat every day. They would only get proper food once in three days. He said that his eldest daughter has seen starvation whereas the daughters who were born after I came here eat well. In ten years great change has taken place in the entire county. Now every family has solar lighting and we have supplied them with a bicycle, an umbrella, something to eat and something to wear.

Sannyasins should leave the cities and come to the villages. They all eat heavy, sweet, tasty food, but a sannyasin, a sadhu, should eat only chapatis without butter. People who eat heavy, sweet, tasty food fall sick and pay heavily to the doctor.

Natural sensitivity

The daily pooja will take place today and a thousand cloves will be offered. Yesterday it was done with hibiscus flowers. Today it will be done with cloves. The Mother is sitting here in Rikhia. Her face is towards the west so I give my pranams from the eastern side, and this should also be the rule for *pradakshina*, walking around the Devi ceremonially.

At this moment the Mother Goddess has already been installed. Even the three Lords Brahma, Vishnu and Maheshwara bow their heads at the feet of the divine Mother. In *Saundarya Lahari* (v. 25) it is said:

> *Trayaanaam devaanaam trigunajanitaanaamapi Shive*
> *Bhavet poojaa poojaa tava charanayoryaa virachitaa*
> *Tathaa hi tvatpaadodvahanamanipeethasya nikate*
> *Sthitaa hyete shashvanmukulitakarottamsamukutaah.*

"The worship of Your feet, O Consort of Shiva, is also worship of the three deities Brahma, Vishnu and Mahesh born of Your three gunas. They require no special worship because they are ever waiting with joined palms held above their diademed heads in salutation to You by the side of the foot-stool of diamonds that bears Your feet."

This is what the scriptures say and She is installed here, yet you are touching my feet. This is peculiar. I do

82

not understand how your devotion is so blunted. Not just for the last three days but for the whole week I have been telling you to forget my feet and also to forget Swami Satyananda. If you love a little here and a little there, then it will be blasphemy. At this moment all your mind should be with Her alone.

Devi, who is the embodiment of emotion, the embodiment of nirguna, the one whom I have installed in my heart as Mother, worship Her at least until the 1st of December. After that wife, child, guru, disciple, whosoever – touch their feet, kiss them if you want to, it doesn't matter. But until then there is only one aim in life and only one obsession, and that is Devi. I have put on socks so that your hands do not touch my feet. At this moment you should be very sensitive. In our relationship with Devi there should be sensitivity. Is there no sensitivity in your relationship with your wife? When we are sensitive with our wife or husband, son or daughter, brother or sister, then why should we not be so with God? The pandits are performing the pooja and if you accept that the divine Mother is here then forget Swami Satyananda sitting here.

Total love

There is a story about a mullah who was performing namaz. A mullah will sit anywhere when the time comes to pray and start calling 'Allaha'. A young girl was in a hurry to meet her boy friend and she walked over the mullah's prayer mat. The mullah became very angry and called out, "You have walked over my sacred mat. Stop stop!" But she didn't stop as, obsessed with her love, she went to meet her boyfriend in the coffee house. The mullah came across her there and said, "How badly misbehaved you are. Didn't you know I was praying?"

"What are you saying?" asked the girl. The mullah replied, "I was praying." "To whom?" she asked. "God, who else!" he said.

Then the girl said, "If you were praying to God, then how did you know I walked over your prayer mat? I did not

83

realize that you were on the mat. I was so obsessed with my love that I did not notice you at all."

Now you know what kind of love you have for your God. So tell me, when you say Mother, how can you remember Swami Satyananda's feet? How can you remember Swami Niranjan's feet? Just imagine that two ordinary people are wandering around. This is called sensitivity, but it has to be natural. The relationship with God should have true sensitivity like the sensitivity you have for your wife or husband, or which you have for the one who is closest to you in life. Do not take your relationship with God and the divine Mother as a formality only. Do not think of them only as images of clay. If you do a ritual automatically and say, "*Aum Namah, Aum Namah, Aum Namah*", then there is no difference between you and the pandits.

Don't take it in the wrong spirit, but God's devotion is a love affair. Everyone has said this. Devotees have said it. Chaitanya Mahaprabhu, Mirabai and all the great Sufi and Christian saints have said it. In the *Narada Bhakti Sutras* it has been said:

> *Saa tvasmin paramaprema swaroopaa.*
> Devotion is nothing but love.

What is the form of bhakti? What is the content of bhakti? What is this bhakti made up of? Total love. Extreme love. When all the love is assembled at one place, then what do we call it? That is called total love, bhakti.

Difference between bhakti and attachment
Love of wife, love of husband, love of son, love of daughter, love for money, this love, that love – all your love when connected to the world is called attachment. The difference between bhakti and attachment is only direction. That is what the saints said about the temperament of divine love and worldly love.

I am trying to explain just one small point. There is no harm in touching my feet. I never objected earlier, but I am

84

objecting at this time. I am objecting to your touching my feet and I am objecting to your relating to me as a guru here. It is not right when the Mother's image has been installed in front of you.

What is the meaning of this existence? What is the meaning of my existence? I believe that the Creator of the world, the divine Mother has come here. Now, at this moment all the devis from Vindhyachal, Vrindavan and Maihar have come here. Become a little sensitive. When you become sensitive then you will feel the vibration of the Devi. But at the moment you are so blunt that you are touching my feet. You have a wife and you are kissing her also, your son is there and you are loving him. From somewhere you get happiness, from somewhere suffering. It is not that you give one mind to this, one mind to that and a third mind to something else. You only have one mind. Put it where you want to put it. If you want to touch feet then touch feet, and if you want to love then do so. No one is going to object. But I take serious objection to your touching my feet during the period of yajna.

Swami Niranjan: The pooja will start soon. Whatever worship you are witnessing is a pure tantric practice. People have a lot of misgivings and for the sake of convenience they talk about left-handed tantra, right-handed tantra, etc., etc. Many names are given, but in tantra the practice of worship is most important. What you are witnessing here is the purest form of tantra, not only pure but purest.

When the program of this Sat Chandi Maha Yajna was being planned, we discussed what should be given in the form of prasad from the Mother and many people expressed their views. Some said to give Sri Yantra, some said vibhooti, some said flowers. When all these thoughts were placed before Sri Swamiji he laughed and said, "Look, you do not understand tantra. It is true that in tantra there is a provision for yantras, mantras, mandalas and different processes. But all these symbols of tantra are transcendental symbols beyond the human mind, beyond the human intellect, where there is always faith. If you give Sri Yantra, what will people see? They will see lines and think that these lines have been given by a fakir. They will keep it, but they will not understand the value of it."

These were Sri Swamiji's words. What you call the Kali Yuga in traditional language, he calls the Computer Age in modern language. The Sri Yantra of this Computer Age is a symbol that automatically generates faith and love. This symbol is that of Rama and Sita. The symbol is of their meeting. There is a unity between atma and paramatma, there is a meeting of consciousness and nature. There is no wife or child but marriage definitely takes place, and that marriage is of atma with paramatma. In that respect no one is a bachelor. Everyone has got married.

There is union in everyone's life and there is separation and pain in everyone's life. Everyone has suffering and everyone has some happiness, and we are all aware of it. Is there no conjunction and separation in your life? Is there no attraction and repulsion? Was there never love in your life? It has definitely happened. This yoga is the most important thing in our life.

This yoga and *viyoga*, union and separation, are the most important events in life. Tantra also talks about yoga and viyoga and, in the Computer Age, the symbol of union and separation, happiness and sorrow, is the marriage of Rama and Sita. That is the Sri Yantra of the Computer Age and also of the Kali Yuga. This symbol, as Sri Yantra and as a blessing of the Mother, will be given to each family and you will be able to understand the system of tantra in that.
Sri Swamiji: We are trying to define something which is beyond the intellect. All the great saints and sages, rishis and prophets, are trying to define something or someone who is beyond the intellect. But the problem is that the one who has to understand it is the intellect. The intellect has to understand someone who is non-intellectual. How can we do it? How can we transform a transcendental matter into an empirical matter? After all, how do you know reality? Reality is not a subject for the intellect.

So people talk about tantra and Sri Yantra sometimes, but what do you know about Sri Yantra? They say, "Here is akasha, here is vayu, here is prithvi, here are devatas, here are devis," but they don't understand anything. A symbol or a yantra has to be something to which you can relate with your intellect. That is why this year, this Sri Yantra of our time – Sita and Rama – will be given. Whether kundalini meets with Shiva in sahasrara or whether jivatma meets paramatma within this body, it is Sita uniting with Sri Rama – that is the most important thing. Therefore, none of you should think that it is some sort of religious symbol that we will be presenting to you this year. This is the Sri Yantra, because marriage is something which everyone can understand because you are all married. You have had all the feelings, you have had all the knowledge, all the experience, mental, emotional and so on, of marriage.

That same experience can take place in spiritual life also. What is the ananda experience? When the jivatma and paramatma unite, when there is a fusion between two forms of consciousness, the little one and the big one, what is the experience? Do you get that through Sri Yantra? No, you get it because you have lived a married life. We are talking of the same experience which is continuous. The experience does not end. The heightened awareness is dhyana, the lightened awareness is spiritual meditation.

Swami Niranjan: You know that when Sri Swamiji first came to this area many people did not have food and clothing.
Sri Swamiji: Nor cigarettes; bidis were not available at all. Now even they are available. If there is no arrangement for bidis, then there is no life for elderly people. No life at all. If there are some puffs and a peg from the bottle, then one can enjoy life. Even an ass can get rotis, water and food, but they don't enjoy bidis. Bidis are something which only human beings can enjoy.
Swami Niranjan: Slowly, Sivananda Math started its activities here with Sri Swamiji's permission. Now one more scheme has been added, called the old age pension scheme.

Sri Swamiji: Not pensioners, co-travellers.

Swami Niranjan: The government announced this scheme but we are running it. Every month all the co-travellers of Sri Swamiji receive fifty rupees and clothes, umbrellas or whatever is required, depending upon the season.

Sri Swamiji: We will all require an umbrella. It will be so hot on the way, and it is such a long way from here to the abode of God. Who knows how many years it will take? On the way we may smoke a few little bidis. If there is money in the pocket then we will eat some nuts as well, because the road is so long. And the biggest thing is that nobody knows the way.

We are travelling to our original home. We are here in this world as visitors for fifty to eighty years, then ultimately we have to return home. So before we go, I thought, "Let me have some money and you had better have some money. On the way we will have a little puff and a drink, something like that!" They are all travellers of between seventy and eighty years and some of them have already gone. They got their ticket and we are still on the waiting list.

Swami Niranjan: So, under this scheme, every month the co-travellers are given different things, according to the season. If it is raining, they are given umbrellas. If it is cold, they are given blankets and sweaters.

Sri Swamiji: Not for here, for there! Because the return journey is very long. We don't even know which way to go. Someone may even forget the road and come back again after five or six years. So sometimes they need umbrellas, sometimes they need shoes and sometimes a little money for the travel abroad, meaning for a broad life. Abroad does not mean going to Europe.

Swami Niranjan: There are quite a large number of co-travellers as you will see and each one is given about five hundred and one rupees every month, along with other accessories to facilitate their travel.

Sri Swamiji: This is the scheme that the government of India announced, but I am implementing it. They have already received their pension for this month. In a very

88

important way, Bhole is really the founder of the whole scheme. He was a dog, but there was a soul inside him who used to give me proper guidance. Before he left his body, he said, "Swamiji, my work is over. I came here to be a companion in your panchagni sadhana and now that work is complete." In panchagni sadhana the devata Bhairava is there, and the dog is Bhairava. Bhole came here for that period and when his work was over he left. So since that day the elderly have received their pension. But now they will receive something extra on the occasion of Sat Chandi Yajna.

Swami Niranjan: Another group which is going to receive prasad are the womenfolk of this area who are known as sakhis. These *sakhis* are actually the companions of Sita during the time of marriage, her attendants. You will see the transformation that takes place in them between today and the last day. They look divine and they walk gracefully, they sing joyously and it is a sight to behold.

Prasad will be given to the builders of the ashram. You see, people who build palaces, houses and homes live in huts and slums! They are the builders, the architects of the comforts which all of you enjoy, but they have no facilities to provide themselves with a proper dwelling. Those people, the labourers, the workers and the masons who have built this entire Alakh Bara campus will also be given prasad of clothing and accessories, of shoes and blankets, implements and tools of construction.

Sri Swamiji: The builder of this place is Yunus Mian Ansari. His masons are all 'Mianjis' – very good builders; they work fast.

Now this year we are going to build an Australian gurukul. We have already received the money. Two to three hundred Australians will stay there. The Italian gurukul is already built, so Italians are staying there. The Colombian cottage is also built.

Swami Niranjan: Finally, the young people of this area, the students who love to enjoy life, who love to play, will be provided with cricket sets.

89

Sri Swamiji: Although cricket is going through a very bad time! The heroes are being reduced to zero! But I give them a cricket set every year. I like cricket but I never played it because I had no time as I had to work for my family.

Swami Niranjan: So now we begin the distribution of prasad to the elderly.

Sri Swamiji: A saint had said, "Fold your bedding, keep your bedding folded in this journey." To believe that this hotel of the world is your home is wrong. We are only visitors here. We come here with a residential permit for seventy to eighty years and now the visa is expiring. Now we are going home. All the preparations are being made. Only the ticket has to be booked. They say there are no seats, all the trains are booked. That's what they are saying.

You are earning the merits of giving. Earn for your whole life and spend a little on your wife and children but not more. Now the clothes, cosmetics and jewellery will be presented to Sita's companions. They are given everything that you would wear when you go to a party. Now the builders will be provided with prasad and with their trade implements by another builder from Greece, who constructed the ashram in Paiania, which is the head-quarters of the yoga movement in Greece.

Swami Satsangi knows all the builders by heart and they know her by heart. Sometimes she regales them with such piercing orders, "Do you want to work or not? If you do not want to work then go away. We have not engaged you to give away forty rupees every day." The whole day they argue and counterargue so loudly. She is well known throughout this area. They are the people to whom your religion denied basic rights, and as a result of that your country has come to this state.

Swami Niranjan: Now gifts of cricket sets will be given to the captains of the Rikhia cricket team.

Sri Swamiji: I hope they will choose their heroes well – Sachin Tendulkar, Ganguli and so on.

Bihar Yoga University

Swami Niranjan: In June this year the Government of India through the University Grants Commission officially and formally declared Bihar Yoga Bharati to be the first yoga university in the world. With this decision we have also been able to fulfil the cherished dream of our paramguru, Swami Sivananda, and the sankalpa of our guru, Swami Satyananda.

Sri Swamiji: Swami Sivananda, my guru, wanted to have a university in Rishikesh. He planned to call it the Yoga Vedanta Forest University. The University Grants Commission advised the ashram committee that it would have to sign over its properties to the university. At that time the committee could not agree, so it did not happen.

When Swami Niranjan pushed the idea of a yoga university, the Grants Commission asked, "Will you offer all your property?" So I said to Swami Niranjan, "It is not our property. Everyone has contributed to the scheme of Bihar School of Yoga. It wasn't formed from my father's income or your father's income, it is everyone's property. So why not say yes?" So we signed the paper and now Bihar School of Yoga, Ganga Darshan, all belong to the university. After that the University Grants Commission gave its permission. That was one thing.

The second thing they said was, "But there is no university that teaches just one subject." I said, "Yoga has many faces: ecology, psychology, philosophy, therapy, medicine etc. We teach four subjects: yoga philosophy, yoga psychology, applied yogic science and yoga ecology, and if necessary we can include Sanskrit as a fifth subject." They were convinced. This is a very good beginning. I hope throughout the world such universities of yoga will emerge, but it is not easy. You need very, very solid and thorough management. Even in this yajna, you can see how the management has been planned. You don't just have buildings and teachers from anywhere and everywhere.

Swami Niranjan: The organization during this Sita Kalyanam, the inner management, was performed entirely by the students of Bihar Yoga Bharati. When you build a house there are many bricks. Bricks are important, but the bonding between the bricks is also important, the cement, the sand, the water. During this program the students of Bihar Yoga Bharati have worked as the bonding agent. Swamis have been the bricks, no doubt, but without the help of the students I am sure that this event would not have been as grand as it is today.

Sri Swamiji: This university is a big achievement. Everyone has worked for it. Everyone at the governmental level and at the ministerial level has put effort into it. All the legal hurdles, procedural hurdles and governmental hurdles have been cleared. The government wanted it and everyone at cabinet level and in the Education Department gave it a push. Otherwise one small hurdle can take a decade to clear among the government departments; the file goes around in circles and comes back. The government has been favourable and they have all helped.

* * *

Yajna and purification

Nowadays the subject of ecology speaks of how to reduce the green house gas effect and global warming, how to neutralize carbon monoxide, but the greatest contribution to ecology will be yajna. Yajna purifies the atmosphere, it purifies the air and special ingredients are mixed in the offering to the yajna. That is why in ancient times kings used to perform yajna on a large scale. Why did they do yajna? For the sake of purifying the atmosphere. So yajna and its effects will also be a research subject in the university.

What is yajna? Is it religious or is it scientific? Nowadays every aspect of our religion is termed religious and is thus denied credibility. In the Vedic religion the customs are actually not sectorial but relate to ecology, to society, to the body, to the neighbourhood and the neighbours. So the customs of yajna also need to be explained so that people can perform yajna in their homes for the purification of the atmosphere. This has been our traditional system.

Avoid politics

Swami Dayananda Saraswati created more awareness of this, but there were a lot of religious confrontations. When religion enters the area of political confrontation its theme is damaged. If any religion adopts a political cause or a sectorial theme, then it gets hurt and people move away from it. So we don't want our people, our sannyasins, to involve themselves in politics.

What is the use of criticizing any religion? If I criticize you, what happens? Just because I call you an owl or an ass or a pig or a thief, you don't become that. Similarly, using critical names does not harm a religion. What we should do is to make all the customs of our religion so simple that, in this Computer Age, if someone has fifteen minutes, he can do something useful with it. Once a week, once a month on full moon day or on the day of the dark moon, people can assemble somwhere for an hour or an hour and a half and do something useful. We have to suggest something like this. Swami Dayananda Saraswati's work in this direction was going well, but it received a big blow. Stepping into politics always gives religion a big blow and ordinary people are scared off.

Know yourself

So this is not an intellectual feast, this is a spiritual feast. The basis of a spiritual feast is your inner feelings, your spiritual and inner receptivity. You imbibe the spirit of this pooja not through understanding but by feeling. Why do they sprinkle water, why do they sing loud or soft, why do they sing that five times? – these are all intellectual questions. Either they have no answer or they have many answers, as many as you can give.

The only pont is that mantra and ritualistic worship, the *karmakanda*, the tantric form of worship, creates a stir, a

93

living movement in the etheric plane, in the plane of energy, a plane where many of us have not reached. Man is not only the little he knows about himself. You are not only what you know about yourself. You only know the tip of the iceberg! What you or I know about ourselves is only the tip of the iceberg.

That infinite atma, that infinite personality, that infinite being that you are, is still hidden from you. It is hidden from me – I don't know myself! That is the tragedy of the human being – we have it but we don't know it.

> *Tera saai tujjha men jyon puhupana men baas*
> *Kasturi kaa miraga jyon puni puni khojai ghaas.*

> Your Lord lives within you
> as the fragrance remains in the flower.
> But man, like the musk deer,
> searches for the scent in the worldly grass.

Like the musk deer, we have everything in us. So it is that inner being which is being stirred by these mantras and rituals. They influence the etheric personality not the conscious mind, not the subconscious mind and not the unconscious mind. We have read about conscious, subconscious and unconscious. Dr Sigmund Freud and others have explained it, but that is just the tip of the iceberg – man extends far beyond the unconscious.

Yajna and turiya

Turiya, the fourth dimension of your personality, is *ananta*, eternal, and *avyaya*, non-decaying. Read the *Mandukya Upanishad*, which defines the dimensions of one's personality. Kabir also says:

> *Bhrikutee mahal ki khabar padee jab aasan aadhar jamaayaa*
> *Jaagrit swapna sushupti jaaneei tureeyaa taar milaayaa*

"After being established in an asana and awakening ajna chakra, waking, dream and deep sleep are transcended and the sadhaka attains turiya."

Then you are not in the earth; you are not even in heaven. You are somewhere in between – *aasan adhar jamaaya*. You place your atma somewhere else, where you don't touch the earth, where you don't touch akasha, space. You don't touch any of the elements and you connect to the cable of turiya.

You have to connect to the subtle, transcendental string of turiya, then nothing else needs to be done. You don't have to do anything, just sit and keep quiet. The noisy band that is making so much disturbance inside has to be silenced. Twenty-four hours a day this loud band is making a noise about my son, my daughter, my uncle, my aunt, my money, my bank, my house – "Alas suffering! Alas happiness! Alas my possessions!" This band which is making such a loud noise has to be silenced for some time. Just keep on saying *Namastasyai Namastasyai Namastasyai Namo Namah* – "Salutations, salutations," and don't try to understand anything. Nothing happens with the brain. Intellect is the barrier, Sri Aurobindo has written this.

Just sit and experience

Ramakrishna Paramahamsa has said that you may write down 'water, water, water' many times, but your thirst will not be taken care of. If we get one glass of water the work is over. It is not necessary to understand God. One has to experience God. It is not necessary to explain God. Will you explain your mother or your father?

This pooja is not an intellectual feast. It is not a matter of intellect or analysis. It is not a matter of understanding or appreciation. It is not a matter of criticism. It is just a matter of acceptance. Either you don't accept it or you do accept it, that's all. Either you accept your father is your father or you just deny him. What is the use of proving he is your father? You can't prove it, unless you undergo a genetic test. In the same way there is no use talking; just sit down quietly. Sometimes the *unmani* or 'no mind' state comes. Sometimes you feel sleepy. All this is okay, it is all right, but keep sitting there.

You have to do something with the mind, at least to some extent. How long will you serve your servant – for the rest of your life? You are only serving your servant. You are a slave of your slave. It is said, "I am a disciple of that saint who controls his mind totally... and that one who can control the mind totally becomes a junior god."

There are many junior gods here. Maybe I am a junior god as well. Who knows? If you cannot control the mind totally, at least slap it and tell it to sit silently. You only have to sit for two hours. After the 1st of December you are free to do anything – watch television, go to the cinema, smoke a bidi, smoke a cigarette, consume liquor, go to a hotel. Who cares? It will all be okay – hotel, bottle, total. But here neither hotel nor bottle nor total is acceptable. Here you have to sit silently for two hours.

Look at our children, the little girls from the village. They sit for such long hours. Can you see how quietly they sit? After all, they also have a mind and they have under-stood one thing, which is that during this time they are allowed to be at Swamiji's place. Otherwise Swamiji never allows entry. By sitting like this, these children have the opportunity to be here for four or five or six hours. Otherwise, they are always told to go home and they are not allowed to come. It is very tempting for them to be here, which is why they sacrifice something and keep silent. They know Swamiji will say, "This child is good. Okay, sit here." If they commit any mischief then they will be sent home, which they do not want.

Invocation of shoonya

Before the arati begins one more thing has to be said. There is no image here. This invocation is of the shoonya for the shoonya. It is the invocation of the attributeless existence for the shoonya. There is no idol and no *murti* or image here. There is no God or demi-God here. We have only invoked the formless into a formless space. We have only invited, we have only invoked, a *nirguna*, formless, placeless, eternal, infinite atma, having no name. We have

96

given Him a name because we are used to it. We have given Her a sex because we are used to it. Otherwise She is neither male nor female. We have invoked Her, and where have we placed It? Somewhere in that space; we don't know where that space is.

We have invited the attributeless Shakti into shoonya. Only a cloth is put around something to represent Her. God can be created anywhere, in water, on earth, in fire, in air, anywhere.

> *Earth, water, fire, air, ether is Ram.*
> *In the heart, mind, prana and senses is Ram.*
> *In the brain, blood, nerves and muscles is Ram.*
> *To the right is Ram, to the left is Ram.*
> *In the front is Ram, over is Ram,*
> *Under is Ram, everywhere is Ram.*
> *Sri Ram Jaya Ram, Jaya, Jaya, Ram.*

Yesterday a thousand offerings were done with cloves and today a thousand offerings will be done with *bel patta*, leaves of the sacred bel tree.

Dancing, kirtan and health

There is only one secret to health. Either you dance in the name of *bhoga*, materialism or you dance to the tune of yoga. One can do silent kirtan or dynamic kirtan where you sing and keep jumping and dancing. We have heard many names like Chaitanya Mahaprabhu, Mirabai and so on. What happens is that God's name purifies the mind. When you jump and dance, that is a kind of elimination; a process of purifying the body sets in. So to purify the body and mind, one should keep on doing kirtan as well as jumping and dancing. Sing:

> *Naache Gopala, sundar laala, naache Sri Hari keertan men.*
> Dance, beautiful Gopala, dance in the Lord's kirtan

Dancing at the time of the Lord's kirtan is an aspect of sadhana, there is an ancient understanding that kirtan is the best way to be close to God, to be near Him.

Master your mind

You don't plan ambitiously on money. You plan on strength, you plan on ability. Plans are made on capacity. You will see then that people from around the world will come to give and they will also come to take. Where there is giving and receiving, it is not termed commerce. Commerce is where you only receive and receive and there is hesitation in giving. Receiving is a nice feeling, but what about giving? When there is giving and receiving, it is not called business. That happens in Rajsooya Yajna. The great king Yudhisthira performed Rajsooya Yajna. Now a king cannot perform Rajsooya Yajna. Why? One who wins a seat in parliament's assembly by any means, he too is a king, but does he win the heart? One who wins the heart is also a king. I am not giving my viewpoint, I am just saying something ordinary. One who wins the seats in assembly and parliament is a king, but the one who wins the heart is a swami.

Swami means one who is one's own master. *Swa* means one's own master. One who rules over oneself is one's own king. Now, at the moment we are not our own masters. At the moment we are servants. Our master is the mind. It is the mind that rules us. Sometimes it makes us talk, sometimes it makes us speak the truth. Sometimes it makes us practise austerities. Sometimes it compels us to steal, sometimes to do charity. Sometimes it makes us adopt the path of righteousness and sometimes the path of unrighteousness. The king is our mind and we are the servants.

When the mind becomes the servant and we become the master, then we are a swami. Swami Vivekananda and others were masters of their minds. Great people make the mind a servant, and the mind can be a good capable worker. If you can make the mind your servant, you can achieve all the subtle capabilities, *siddhis*, and all the divine blessings or *vibhootis,* which come from the mind. Now the mind is enjoying the position of the guru, and that is why it does not do anything.

Daan Yajna

The important point is that here we do not give gifts. We do not give donations either. We only give prasad. Whatever sari, shawl, T-shirt or other item you have received is not a gift. *Prasad* means that which is offered to God. Prasad is from the hands of the Almighty Lord. When a mother feeds her child, it is alright even if she gives him her own morsel of food. When the child has a fever the mother covers him with her own blanket. Now, if the child says that he wants a new blanket, then that child is stupid. Imagine, the child is sick and the mother is giving him her blanket. The blanket is old, so then the child says he wants a new one and criticizes the blanket that his mother has just given to him.

This is exactly the relationship that exists between you and your divine Mother. If She gives you an old, ragged blanket, you take it. And if, instead of a blanket, She gives you old and torn clothes stitched together, what then? And suppose She doesn't give you anything at all. Maybe She doesn't wish to. So our relationship with God is something different.

Swami Niranjan: As Sri Swamiji has said, one aspect of the yajna is being conducted by the pandits. The second aspect of yajna is the prasad yajna, and it is equally important. It is not only recitation of mantra which is necessary, the prasad yajna is also important. This is known as Daan Yajna, donating something with devotion. Mother is being worshipped not only through the recitation of *Durga Saptashati*, but in this form of worship when everyone receives the warm blessings of Mother's protection. The whole world is embodied and exists in Her warm affectionate being. Giving is also a part of the yajna, so do not think, "These people are doing their work, now let me slip away." No, continue to sit with the same devotion that you felt during the chanting.

Bhole

There was a palm tree here and a boy used to climb it every week for country liquor. He made a business out of country liquor. I used to live in the akhara and Bhole would bark loudly. He couldn't climb the tree, but he would keep walking and jumping on his hind legs. I told the boy not to come or else Bhole would go mad. Seeing him, Bhole would become uncontrollable. He has bitten all the swamis. People did not want to go near that kutir, even if there was work there, because everyone was seized with fear of Bhole. Day or night, whatever urgent work called them, nobody dared to go to Ganesha Kutir, so great was their fear of him. At last I had the tree cut down and I gave the boy an autorickshaw to get rid of this problem. Otherwise every evening Bhole would lay in wait for him.

My anushthana ended in 1999 on the day of Devotthan Ekadasi. Not long after that Bhole came near my feet, which was his normal practice, and did not get up at all. He always used to rub himself against my feet. He did it two or three times and then he lay down and did not get up. This is called 'death by wish', voluntary death. His work was over. There are many people who come here with a purpose and when the purpose is over they go, like Vivekananda, Shankaracharya and Jnaneshwar. People like us are just alive without purpose.

Swami Niranjan: Sri Swamiji was telling us about Bhole, his companion. Many of you know that Bhole came here at the time when Sri Swamiji was performing his panchagni sadhana. Bhole was not just a dog, rather he was a spirit incarnate in the body of a dog, and had come for a special purpose. The year Sri Swamiji finished his sadhana after ten years, Devotthan Ekadashi took place on the 16th of November. *Devotthan* means 'the gods are awakening'. After that, Bhole came to Sri Swamiji one evening, rubbed his head against him two or three times, then lay down at his feet and quietly went to his eternal sleep.

100

That indicates a certain quality. Those people and those spirits who incarnate with a purpose also choose the time of their departure. There are such people in history who have chosen the time when they will leave this mortal frame. Many saints and enlightened beings have done it, many ordinary people have also done it and Bhole also chose his time. The purpose, the reason, for his being with Sri Swamiji was over when the sadhana was over.

Most of you know about Bhole. Although he was externally ferocious, internally he was one with Sri Swamiji. And believe me, he used to communicate. His eyes used to communicate, his mouth used to communicate his feelings, his emotions, his *bhava*. So in his memory, the old age pension is given to all the elderly of the area on that day.

When Bhole first came, about twelve years ago, Sri Swamiji said, "Bhole has the blessing of Lakshmi, the goddess of wealth," and he named the store where we keep the prasad for the people of Rikhia 'Bhole's Readymade Store'. Since that day that store has never been empty.

Sri Swamiji: You empty it in the morning and it is full again in the evening.

Lakshmi ke bhandaara kee baree apooraba baata
Jyon kharache tyon tyon barhe bin kharache ghata jaata.

"Lakshmi's storehouse is very peculiar. It increases as you empty it and decreases if not emptied."

Swami Niranjan: We came here one month ago and the storeroom was full up to the roof. Then before the beginning of Sat Chandi, whatever was in the storehouse was distributed amongst two counties. Previously we used to say that Sri Swamiji had adopted only the Rikhia county. But this year two counties have been adopted. So ten days ago we cleaned out the storeroom, but in the last eight days that room has been totally filled up again.

Sri Swamiji: That is why we have made a tomb for Bhole. There is a Bhole samadhi and on it I have not written "Dog". I have said, "In memory of Bhole, the faithful companion during Panchagni." So you would not know him as

101

a dog. You would call him a disciple. Dog was only the name of the body; the soul was not of a dog.

Vidhyaarinayasampanne braahmane gavi hastini
Shuni chaiva shvapaake cha panditaah samadarshinah.

"Sages look with equal vision on a Brahman endowed with learning and humility, on a cow, on an elephant, and even on a dog and an outcaste."

This is written in the *Gita* (5:18). The soul is the same, even in a dog, and I recognized his soul.

* * *

The energy field of yajna

Participation in yajna is very important because it creates an energy field. Divine power is created, and so long as you recite the mantra, you do not hear the sound of that loud band inside you. This is an advantage but not a total advantage. By mantra recitation, energy is created in the subtle consciousness. There are good environments and there are bad environments, which you know and it is not necessary to explain it. That energy takes care of our karmas, dharmas, mistakes and sickness. And at that time the tenth gate is closed.

In this bungalow of the body there are nine gates. The tenth gate is locked with a key and the gate keeper, the *chetan purusha*, the subtle consciousness, does not allow anyone in just as we do not allow anyone in here. He stops everyone. If the tenth gate opens a bit, then Kabir says, "For one who meditates on that supreme purusha the game of karmas, illusions, diseases and mistakes that we have been playing is dispelled."

All the bad debts are written off and then a new life begins. Now from today we can start a new loan account. We can all do this. We go home having washed off everything and then we start borrowing again.

You won't see this kind of yajna anywhere else. In this yajna the process of Vedic Sanatan Dharma has been

102

adopted. Nothing is lacking in it yet we have adopted the management process of the modern Western world as well and we have made a synthesis of both disciplines.

* * *

The tradition of Karna's generosity

In ancient times the site of the ashram in Munger was called Karna Chaura. Duryodhana had made his friend Karna the governor of Anga Desh. His palace once stood on the site of the present Ganga Darshan ashram. Close by is the temple of the goddess Chandi, where Karna used to perform yajna followed by havan and then give gold to the brahmins. In those days the brahmins were poor. Nowadays the brahmins are cobblers in Bata and ironsmiths in Tata! But in those days they were very poor and lived only on alms.

When I came here to Rikhia, I thought, "Let this be Karna Chaura. Instead of giving gold we will give clothes." Recently we received a truck from Orissa. Sometimes we get clothes or blankets from here and there, so our work goes on and we distribute them in the villages. Altogether in a year we give Good Luck kits to about two hundred girls. I thought, "Although I have not married, I can surely give dowries."

Today you have seen the boys and girls of Rikhia. You should have seen them before. During the day no one would pass this way. Nowadays at least fifty to a hundred scooters pass by. Qualification is one thing, ability is another, but one thing is sure, when someone gets the blessing of God that person becomes someone. We understand that without the grace of God and without blessings, knowledge alone does not give success in life. That is what I used to tell the people of the village. So we just worship God and here we believe one more thing.

Rahiman chup hvai baithiye dekhee dinan ke pher
Jab neeke din aaihai banat na lagihain der.

You should keep quiet when you are passing
through bad periods.
When good times come things click very fast.

Grace

May good days come in our human life. Man has only one
resource available to change destiny, and that is the grace
of God. Once he is able to stir God's grace, then the destiny
of a man changes; the dacoit becomes a saint, the pauper
becomes a king and the blind shows the world the way, like
Surdas, who gave the eye of wisdom to the world. So you
are fine wherever you are, but also find the way to receive
the blessings of God. The best way to receive them is to go
peacefully to the place where God's bhajan and kirtan is
taking place. And here you will get it in abundance.

Rural development

In two years we have seen the scene change. Before, girls of
ten and thirteen years were present here. Now they are grown
up girls of eighteen or twenty years because I have been
insisting, "No marriage at that age." Now there are a few
young ones, but the percentage has changed. We suggest
there should only be marriage when the girl is suitable for
marriage. Why will you marry her off uselessly? Give her in
marriage after she is seventeen or eighteen years of age,
when she becomes more mature and some understanding
develops, and when the boy starts earning. Neither the boy
nor the girl earns, yet they get moved around like little
statues.

Now in Rikhia we have employment plans for all the
women, incuding carpentry, electrical work and farm work
with the newest methods. There will be work for old women
and education for little girls. There should be some art and
attainment possible for women and girls, something for
poor working women and girls too, and then the bidi making
will come to a stop here.

There is good news from the Secretary of the Directorate
of the Tourist Department of India. Here in Rikhia, nearby,

104

a tourist bungalow is being constructed. It is a program involving seven hundred thousand rupees. A hundred people will be able to sleep there and it will remain full for the entire twelve months.

We are working for rural development and all the work will be done first for Rikhia county. Of course the whole of India is our county, but once we start here others will also understand how good work for humanity is possible through yajnas and how good people from far away places meet each other at yajnas. Those who cannot come by train will use the airstrip which is being planned for Rikhia? Nearby an airconditioned tourist complex is being built. Many people don't come here because facilities are lacking. Many people cannot stay in the Deoghar hotels. They have been wanting to come here for many years, but they are not prepared to stay in Deoghar at present. They will only come if there are separate arrangements, and it is necessary to bring such people.

November 29, 2000

Sita as kundalini

Sita was born out of earth. The basic element of mooladhara is earth. The same Sita is kundalini and this awakens many times. She travels to *swadhisthana,* which means 'one's own house'. She sleeps in mooladhara, swadhisthana is her home and from there she travels upwards. Upon reaching the top she stays for some time with Rama and Shiva and then returns. She descends, raining nectar all around. The same thing happens with yogis. A yogi's kundalini also falls down. Shankaracharya speaks of the ambrosial flow raining nectar and delusion in his hymn to Devi, *Saundarya Lahari* (v. 10):

Sudhaadhaaraasaaraishcharanayugalaantarvigalitaih
Prapancham sinchanti punarapi rasaamnaayamahasah.
Avaapya svaam bhoomim bhujaganibhamadhyushtavalayam
Svamaatmaanam kritvaa svapishi kulakunde kuharini.

105

"Having drenched the pathway of nadis with the streaming shower of nectar flowing from Your feet, having resumed Your own position after descending from the resplendent lunar regions, and assuming Your form of a serpent with three and half coils, You sleep in the hollow of the kulakund."

What does strengthening delusion mean? Kundalini ascends and then it goes down to earth thereafter. Didn't Sita return alone? Didn't she descend into the earth? We know the kundalini sleeps in that cave. This is the birth of Sita from the earth and this is what is meant by her returning into it. Do not think ill of Rama, believing that he left Sita like that.

Celebration of Sita and Rama's marriage

On the marriage day the pooja will begin in the morning at six and will continue without a break. There will be Kanya Pooja. There are not only nine virgin girls this year but quite a few others. We have taken one girl from every family for the sake of representation. So all the rituals will be performed. There will be pooja, arati, their feet will be washed, they will be offered food, then gifts will be given. Everybody should be present for *poornahuti*, the final offering in the worship, and then we will present each of those hundred and fifty brides with a Good Luck kit from you.

There are clothes for the bride and bridegroom and items for beautification, although I have made it seventeen in place of the traditional sixteen items because in those days tampons were not available. These days we give tampons. Plus some gold or silver or pearls or diamonds or whatever is there.

Thereafter the marriage of Rama and Sita will take place, which means we will make mooladhara meet sahasrara on that day. Please do not fast on the day of the marriage. We are the marriage party and the people of the marriage party eat. Even those who have been observing a fruit diet or light diet should not fast on the marriage day.

106

Some people told me to close the kitchen. I said, "This is the day of marriage! On the marriage day there is a feast. If you close the kitchen on that day then it might as well remain closed for ever." No, on that day the kitchen will be working. But of course you should maintain one restraint. Don't go out and eat rubbish.

Child marriages

Such young girls are given in marriage. They don't even know their own names, but the village chief pushes them to come forward. What do little girls of twelve or thirteen years old understand? They are given in marriage at such an early age.

My approach is not to interfere in another's system because I do not want to become a reformer. A reformer is one who interferes. I do not interfere, rather I suggest. I suggest, "Look, do not do it like that, do it like this." But circumstances in low caste areas are such that they have to give girls in marriage at an early age, otherwise there are a lot of complications. Anything can happen in their family. Lower caste people are very insecure, so they marry off their daughters at an early age and send them to the bridegroom's place.

The genetic factor

Now we take a subtle view of it. The girl representing Sitaji is from Kerala and Rama is from Bengal. We have always said that marriage should span great distances. The genetic factor should be kept in view, because if marriage takes place between maternal or paternal brothers and sisters then the genetic law is not maintained. Diseases like polio or blindness can be due to genetic factors. This genetic factor is omnipresent.

These days there is yet another disease where HIV becomes positive and AIDS strikes. These things are increasing because today relationships are based on loose morals. If a boy falls in love with a girl, marriage takes place. This does not matter to me. In matters of love and

107

war nothing is taken to be wrong, but nowadays we arrange marriages only where there is some connection of positive and negative between the boy and girl.

In English we call this genetics and here we call it *sagotra*, the same genetic group, and *agotra*, a different genetic group. Marriage should not be within one *gotra*, one genetic group. The genetic batch should be different for at least to seven generations; only then will the children be of good quality. The quality of health will also be good then. Many diseases occur on account of the DNA factor, like diabetes. Is there any treatment for diabetes? Ask the doctors. Diseases which occur due to non-scientific matching of sexual relationships cannot be treated.

* * *

Prasad

Swami Niranjan: You all come here and Sri Swamiji's gates are open. Everyone receives something, at least blessings. No one leaves empty-handed, remember this. This is the place of the divine Mother and the blessing of the universal Mother, the divine energy, is being invoked here, so how can you go back empty-handed? You are getting love, always keep this in mind.

God has created this entire universe; the entire cosmos, the entire *srishti*, creation, is His. The fruit that we eat is manufactured by God. The water we drink comes from the factory of creation. After all, everything is God's gift to us and when we offer fruits and flowers, we are offering back the same things that God has given us. When we offer these to God it becomes an act of devotion, an act of faith. Similarly, all of you have given many things to Sri Swamiji and now you are receiving things on behalf of Sri Swamiji, and that is an act of love and devotion.

When you connect with God it is devotion, and when you are connected with other people, with other beings, then it is love. So remember that two acts are being performed here: the act of devotion and the act of love.

108

This is what this whole yajna represents. Without love and without devotion any effort is incomplete; all efforts are incomplete.

Master of the mind

Until now you have been a servant, a slave of your own desires and whims and fancies and mind. The mind says, "The body is aching," so you begin to move. The mind says, "I am feeling cold," so you put on warm clothes. The mind says, "I am feeling hot," so you begin to take off your clothes. The mind says, "Dance", so you dance. What is all this? One day, say to your mind, "Be quiet. Today I am the ruler, today you will obey me." Then you will be able to sit from six in the morning to four in the evening to witness the culmination of Sat Chandi Maha Yajna and the union of Sri Rama with Sita.

There are definitely some physical needs which you cannot and should not ignore, otherwise it will be very difficult. Rikhia doesn't have proper medical facilities if your bladder bursts! So there are some physical necessities which we have to consider, but as soon as those needs are fulfilled, come back. Be the ruler, the swami of yourself, for one day.

The bhakti connection is not limited to offering fruits or flowers; in bhakti we offer our lives as well. Our relationship with God is called bhakti. Similarly, once one person gives to another person that is a connection of love. And when a saint, a sadhu, a sannyasin or a higher soul gives something to someone it is called prasad. It is the same thing, whether we call it love or prasad. Not only the have not's but the have's also receive the gift of love. And this too is a worship. This is not business or commerce but worship, and it should be viewed as worship.

Sri Swamiji: It is also a hint to society and also a hint to those who have about what they can do for those who have not. It is also a hint to sannyasins in India. A sannyasin's main duty is to preach spirituality, but during a period of emergency, as it is these days, sannyasins have to enlarge

109

their role. Ashrams will have to become dynamic centres for helping others – that is a hint, that's all.

Swami Niranjan: There was absolute poverty here. People had nothing, nothing in its true sense. The elders here had maybe one and a half dhotis, which they would wash at night and wear again in the morning. Throughout this entire region there were houses where the fire in the kitchen would not burn for three or four days because there was nothing for them to cook. Most people have no idea what such hunger pangs are like.

Sri Swamiji: Even I had no idea. It was my dog, Bhole, who told me. He could communicate with me. His body was that of a dog, just as you have the body of a human being, but some invisible soul had inherited him after he came here. I am not a dog lover. I don't like dogs at all. I like that adage of Rajneesh's: "Dogs and politicians not permitted here." But somehow things transpired in such a way that he had to stay here. Even though I did not like dogs and I still don't, he stayed. That invisible helper, that invisible soul, inherited him. In 1990 I started my panchagni sadhana on Makar Sankranti, the 14th of January. On the 16th of July, six months later, I heard a clear voice, a clear mandate about this. I knew that the dog had been inherited by some benign soul with compassion, with feelings of mercy, with the feeling of atmabhava for all.

Give to others

Everybody experiences his own pain. The pain of others is felt by God alone, not humans.

Apne apne gharan ke sab kahoo ko peer.
Tumhe peer sab gharan kee dhanya dhanya raghubeer.

Everybody has anxiety for their own home
But you, Raghubir have that anxious care for all homes.
You are great, you are great.

God experiences the pain of every home and this was the kind of soul he inherited. That day he hinted to me many,

110

many times, "You have a hut, these people have nothing. You have blankets, they have nothing. You eat once a day because that's all you need. But there are children in some homes who also eat only once but who need food twice or thrice a day. A child needs milk and this and that."

I have never seen their households. I have not met the hungry child. I do not even know whether the child survives or dies. I have not seen the wife, child, or hearth, but my nature has changed. Now I feel that there is only one meaning of life, and that is living for others. We are not strangers here. I have never lived for my fellow beings because no one is my own. They do not belong to me, no one is mine.

Visitors in a foreign land

Why is no one ours? Because we live in a foreign land. This world of mankind is a foreign land. We are visitors here for fifty or eighty years. This is not our home.

> *Rahnaa nahin desh biraanaa hai*
> *Yah sansaar kagad ki puria*
> *Bund pare ghul jaanaa hai*
> *Yah sansaar kanton ki bari*
> *Ulajh pulajh mari jaanaa hai*
> *Yah sansaar jhaar auru jhaankad*
> *Aag lage bari jaana hai*
> *Kahat Kabir suno bhai sadho*
> *Satguru nam thikara hai.*

Don't live here, it's a foreign land.
This world is like a stack of paper.
It will melt away if water drops fall on it.
This world is a bush of thorns.
One who falls in it is entangled and ultimately dies.
This world is just wood and bush.
With the touch of fire it ignites.
Kabir says to the saints, "Listen brothers,
Only the Name of Satguru is our abode."

111

This is not our home. We have only come here as visitors. We are residents of a different world and that is where we have to return to. We do not just believe this, we know this. The seed of man does not belong to this earth. The seed of man belongs to a greater planet. From there, due to his karma, or his error, or for some other purpose, or due to God's will, he has somehow descended to this earthly plane where birth and death is the regular law of life, where one has to search for immortality. Here we have to search for immortality, whereas immortality is our inherent nature. We are immortal. Do we die? Isn't it only the body that dies? We never die. But when someone in this world dies we weep, and when someone in this world survives that makes us happy.

Live for others

So now to live only for others should be the dharma of Swami Satyananda's life. Since the day this thought came to my mind, I have achieved the aim for which I left my home, fifty or sixty years ago. I did tantra, sadhana, I did everything. I read a lot, travelled around the whole world, saw all the temples of Christians, Muslims, Iranians and Parsis. But now I do hear the voice of God. Still, if I want to talk to Him I do not know His telephone number. I asked for His password and He said, "Not yet, lest you commit cyber crime." I am not joking. Sometimes I tell you very serious things jokingly. Sometimes saints and siddhas also commit cyber crimes. But nowadays repeatedly we talk about everything.

Shreya and preya

In this relationship, according to the *Gita* there should be mutual feeling and exchanges, only then will you get the transcendental gains or *shreya,* which means spiritual benefit, spiritual gift or spiritual boon. The path of *preya* takes one to indulgence and the path of shreya takes one to Godhood. The *Kathopanishad* (1:2:2) explains this in the following lines:

112

Shreyashcha preyashcha manushyametastau
Sampareetya vivinakti dheerah,
Shreyo hi dheero'bhi preyaso vrineete
Preyo mando yogakshemaad vrineete.

"The joyful and pleasurable lie before man. The wise man, after discriminating and examining them well, prefers the joyful, but the ignorant, due to greed and attachment, chooses the pleasurable."

The *Kathopanishad* says there are two paths, one path is shreya and the other is preya. You are already on the path of preya, but I want to bring you to the path of shreya. There is no one to help a poor soul. Except for God, there is no one for poor people. It is not right to say that the government belongs to the poor, or society belongs to the poor, or big social places belong to the poor. In this world there is no one to look after poor people but God. We all are strangers to them. No one cares for their welfare. They do not trust anyone; they fear a lot.

I am just living to teach spiritual life. I have applied for a booking. My seat is not booked yet. Once it is booked I will leave this body and go back to my original home from where I came.

Swami Niranjan: You have all been blessed by the darshan of this yajna in the presence of Sri Swamiji. Have no other expectation. There will no interviews. Many of you keep asking, "When can I see Swamiji for one or two minutes, personally, privately." Please remember that if Sri Swamiji was meant to be doing that he would still be in Munger. He has come here for a different reason, so do not expect anything.

Everybody, Indians and overseas guests, will have to leave here by five o'clock the day after tomorrow evening. Don't knock on the door when the program finishes on the 1st and don't come back again on the 2nd, thinking, pondering, with the desire to have darshan of Sri Swamiji and receive his blessings and his satsang. He had given his

113

instruction on the first day for the upliftment of the spiritual life of a person and for his progress. Whether you remember or not I don't know, but he has told you clearly, "This is my order: work for others, not for your own spiritual salvation."

When Sri Swamiji has told us so clearly, we can only pray to God that one who has ears should listen and one who has eyes should see. What more can be said? Therefore, when the program finishes, depart having received the blessings of the Mother and of Sri Swamiji. Say *Namo Narayana* and return to your home. I believe that Sri Swamiji will give us a chance to meet him again sometime, and when it happens we will all come together once more.

* * *

Sri Swamiji: Now the pandits are chanting from the Sama Veda, then they will chant from the Shukla Yajur Veda. People from South India belong to the Krishna Yajur Veda sect. Here in the north it is different. Our relationship with this priest dates from the time when he was a boy. He belongs to a very high category of priests, not an ordinary commercial group.

Sanskrit

I am a great critic of Sanskrit. I understand the differences in the pronunciation of the Sanskrit letters when chanting and I have studied Sanskrit grammar and literature. Our language is Sanskrit. I make mistakes when I speak English, but when I speak Sanskrit I make no mistakes. Now nobody listens to Sanskrit, but this language will grow in importance during this computer period which is coming up. With computers, negative language is used, but if people start using positive language many obstacles will be removed.

In India we have established the relationship of the Sanskrit language with religion, otherwise there is no relationship between language and a particular religion. If we think about it we can see that the language and the religion are different: Urdu and Islam, Latin and

114

Christianity, Sanskrit and Hinduism. Because of this the Sanskrit language is facing difficulties. What relationship has Sanskrit with religion? It makes our language neat and completely clear.

When we write in English, 'p' can be pronounced 'pa'. In *Devanagri*, the script for Sanskrit, it is not like that. When we write the letter 'p', we also pronounce 'p' exactly; the sound is only and exactly that much. This is a difference in phonetics which will be important in the future when computer scientists come to understand the system.

In the Roman script of the English language one letter of the alphabet can have different sounds. In the word 'circus', one 'c' corresponds to the Sanskrit letter 'sa' and the other to the Sanskrit letter 'ka'. You may say circus or kerkash, kershus or sershus. In the Sanskrit system a letter of the alphabet indicates a particular sound. In English, the letter of the alphabet and the word are often different.

Science of vibrations

So these sounds, vibrations, words, letters of the alphabet are different things. From this we learn about two things, sound and the letters of the alphabet. The letters 'k', 'ka', 'ke' or 'ki' that we read produce vibration. We call them *varna*; they have sound and colour. Sanskrit includes the study of how this sound is produced. Whether the sound happens from the throat, nose, teeth, lips or from the palate is included in the structure of the alphabet. With that information the efficiency of computers will increase to a great extent.

Computer science is facing great difficulties. If voice recognition with computers becomes easy then when you push a button you will get the answer. Now, after pushing the button it takes one or two seconds to get the answer; that will all end. For example, now I am talking in your language and you do not need time to understand it. But if I speak in Latin or Sanskrit then you do need time to understand what I am saying. Anyway, English is now the language of the supreme kings so we have to accept it. This is the custom of the world. The person who has the power will enter the market forcibly.

Free science from religion

Now everything will be exposed in front of science. Science has started accepting many things which these people had rejected in the name of religion. Earlier people used to think of yoga as a religion and reject it, but science has recognized its worth and accepted it.

Ayurveda is slowly being accepted because Ayurveda is based on natural things. Although its techniques are chemical techniques, they concern the nature of the gunas. Ayurveda is of a very high quality, but now it has the label of the Hindu religion on it. There should be no label of religion on any science or on politics because science and politics are not concerned with religion. Is biology Christian? Is physics Christian? Science has no relationship with religion.

Now what is the relationship between Sanskrit and the Hindu religion? What is the relationship of Persian with Islam? There is no relationship. So now at last Sanskrit and Ayurveda will be gradually elevated by scientists and those whose minds are opening, because they are adopting new techniques.

For thousands of years *neem*, a medicinal tree, was worshiped here. Now people are making antiseptic products, insecticides and pesticides from neem. They have started making antibiotics from tulsi and in Haridwar there is an antibiotic factory. Today there are forests of tulsi; it is being grown in abundance. Now what is the relationship of tulsi with the Hindu religion? It is a medicine, and medicine is a form of God because it has the power of God. Now, because tulsi has a relationship with the Hindu religion a Christian will not accept it, but a time will come when his priest will take antibiotics prepared from tulsi. There are so many things like that related to science, and gradually we are gradually bringing those things to light.

116

Changes in consciousness

Those people chant Sanskrit so well that you must have perceived *bhrahmaranada*. The black bee makes a sound while moving from flower to flower and the same sound is known as bhrahmaranada. In bhramari pranayama the important part is listening to the sound. With Sanskrit mantras too, listen to them, and even if you don't understand the mantras there will be a chemical and electrical reaction in your brain. There will be a reaction in those beta and alpha waves that you studied at school. There is change that is not seen, and you experience spiritual benefits too. Through spiritual experience you can know atma, the self. Chemical and electrical impulses can be explained, but there will be a change in spirit, a change in consciousness. You have experienced changes in consciousness, haven't you? When you are deceived, when someone dies, on becoming happy, while living your life, is there no change in consciousness? It can be experienced.

Changing destiny

Besides this there is another factor called destiny. Does the egg come from the chicken or the chicken from the egg? The egg comes from the hen and the hen comes from the egg. Man also comes from an egg; that is called destiny. Every action has a fixed result; the result is destined and everyone is under the control of destiny. All of us who are composed of the five elements, who are born from our mother's womb, are under the control of destiny. Why? Because you perform action and no action is without fruit. It may be any physical or mental action, but whatever action you do through the mind has a result. No action is without reaction and everywhere the fruit of action is fixed. Whether you can see it or not, action bears fruit.

That destiny can be changed also through the power of mantra. But before destiny is changed through mantra, there is a rule. We drink liquor and get tuberculosis. We smoke bidis and cigarettes and get cancer. If we have loose

117

morals, we suffer an increased risk of catching AIDS. Now, consider that we prayed and through mantra our disease was cured. For the time being that suffering ended. But if the same lifestyle continues and the suffering comes again, mantra will not cure it. Then no one will be able to cure it. After changing the law, even if God comes you will not be cured, because once the natural flow of karma was stopped through mantra it changed. The law was clear but a higher authority decided something different for you. However, after that you did not fulfil your promises to offer something in return.

Asking and promising

There are two points: to ask and to promise. In 1963 I made a promise in Trayambakeswar and in 1983 I fulfilled that promise. My guru said, "Spread yoga everywhere in the world." It didn't seem to me that I could do it. A small man and such a big world. Where would I work? I thought, "Nobody is ready to listen to me. Even if I publish books, no one will read them." So I said to my Ishta, "The day I have fulfilled this debt of duty to my guru, I will leave everything and come under your protection."

The success that I had within twenty years has not been achieved by any sannyasin to this day. I was able to move like a bulldozer through every country I visited and the girls and boys all had their heads shaved. No one had the courage to speak against it. Once the Pope enquired, "If yoga is a culture of the East, how will you bring the culture of the East to the West?" I replied, "Just like it was done two thousand years ago, because Christianity is also Eastern. Christianity is not the natural religion of Europe, it is an imported religion. So we can fit in like Christianity fitted in two thousand years ago." He didn't have an answer to that.

Give something worth giving

Then in 1983 I left all those things I had taken with me, clothes and watch, at Trayambakeswar. When we suffer we think, "God, let my wishes be fulfilled and I will offer you prasad worth three rupees." No, cheap trade with God is wrong. "I will offer bel leaves, flowers, fruits, one or two litres of milk." No, we are answerable for the blessings that God has given us. When He made you free from such great pain, leave home. What is there in a home? He also changed the rule.

> *Prabal prem ke paale par kar*
> *Prabhu ko niyama dadalate dekha*
> *Apanaa maan bhale tala jave*
> *Jan kaa maan na talate dekha*

> Being won by the intense love of a devotee
> The Lord is seen changing His rules
> His own credit may fall at stake but
> He will never allow any damage
> To the credit of a devotee.

Such a great thing is given to you and what do you give in return? You throw Him two paise, or the milk, fruit and sweets that He has given to you. Offer Him something which is at least at a similar level to that divine grace, if not equal to it.

He gave us the empire of the world. In every country good schools have been opened and sannyasins have been prepared. In every country good teachers have been trained and research has started. Well educated people have started a campaign. This is an empire, isn't it? He has given us such a big empire. What should we give to Him? To just go and offer Him a silken sheet at Trayambakeswar is so cheap!

God is also clever. Everything disappeared in one night. All the enjoyments that He had given disappeared. He who causes destruction through His eyebrow, how much time will He take to destroy the establishment of yoga? God is the power and what are we in front of Him? Our success is all His grace.

God has given us good health. He has given our mind. This is His kindness. Without His grace we cannot become good, without His blessings we are nothing. So I am giving a little hint to any person who is desiring something – don't just give four or five rupees.

Give your life – sannyasa

There is so much power in mantra. In ancient times wars were fought through mantra. Now people have forgotten that there is a lot of power in mantra, whether it is used for offspring, property, employment, salvation, obeying religious duties or dharma, conflict between men and women or making friends. The suffering of many people can be relieved, it can all be removed, if only you ask for God's blessings.

In return why not say, "We will shave our heads and live in Munger for two years like sannyasins." A man goes to prison and then becomes sick. Why doesn't he become a monk? Where is the problem in shaving the head? When we were born we had no hair and the day we go it will be the same. The Adi Shankaracharya sings about this in *Mohamudgara*:

> *Angam galitam palitam mundan dashana viheenam jaatam tundam*
> *Vriddho yaati griheetvaa dandam tadapi na munchati aashaa-pindam.*

"The old man's limbs have decayed, his head is covered with white hairs. His mouth is without teeth and he walks aided by a stick – but still he has not lost his bundle of desires."

At the age of eighty or ninety years, there will be no teeth in your mouth, no hair on your head and your condition will be the same as a small child who cannot sit or stand. Learn to give to God, and give Him something so that He can say, "Well, my son should be like that! I gave him two and he gave me four."

Yoga in Europe

Swami Janakananda from Sweden studied with me in Munger. Then he started working in Europe. I used to come and go. He opened an ashram and acquired a very big building in a traffic free area. In their country there are roads called pedestrian malls where cars are prohibited. They are big roads, not small lanes, but there are so many people that traffic is not allowed. It had a very nice feeling as there was no traffic noise.

He had great success and also published a magazine called *Bindu*. It was a very popular magazine because in it he revealed the science of pranayama in detail: how inhalation and exhalation should be performed and whether the ratio of inhalation and exhalation should be 1:2, 1:4 or 1:6. He would give the opinion of this yogi and that yogi on breath retention and what the ratio of inhalation and retention should be. He would explain it all in detail. They are doing a very good job.

People from far away countries, belonging to a different race and religion, take sannyasa and live in their own countries, like Norway, Denmark and Finland. Scandinavian countries are very peaceful. People speak very politely and they are neat and clean. Men and women are permitted to live together over there and nobody complains. It is not like here. A man and woman living together is common over there. It is called common marriage.

Sexuality and health

I want to tell you that total health includes body, mind, emotions and nature. There is health in nature also. There are many dimensions of health. It is not only a matter of disease. When you talk about health you must also talk about man's nature. Your health and your disease are both parts of your nature. Crying about little things is also a disease. So for total health there is nothing better than yoga. In America, Europe and other countries they have formed the opinion that for the total health of a person one needs asana, pranayama, yoga nidra, pratyahara and dhyana. They have also added the sexual relationship between a man and woman, which is in tantra. They have said that this is included in the basis of health.

The magazine published by Swami Janakananda is read by many people. It has very good sales because Western culture is not a controlled sexual culture. Western culture is a free sex culture. If you purchase chocolate from a shop, there is nobody to stop you. If you have tea in a shop, there is nobody to stop you. If you go to a shop and buy bidis or cigars, there is nobody to stop you. That is called freedom. I am not calling it clean, I am calling it free.

How can these races and cultures spiritualize their free culture? Many of you know magic and witchcraft. Therefore, we know a little tantra, a very little. Tantra is a very great science. It includes diet, drinks, sleep, marriage, children and worship. We have sixty-four tantras here, and they are all prevalent over there.

There are mahamandaleshwars too who were invited to Australia. They travelled throughout the country and took classes to make people understand that life is a process. Eating is a process, sleeping is a process, marriage is a process, giving birth to children is also a process, hatred and love is a process, pain and pleasure is also a process. How can you make it qualitative? How can you spiritualize every action? Today the whole of Europe and America is researching that. Those people are not in search of money like you are. Here people see money in everything, but there people see a life of spirituality in everything.

Governments and yoga in Europe
I used to go abroad very often. In Sweden I was invited by the Department of Education and in many countries the big companies sponsored my visits. I would travel from India like a king, in first class with a secretary. They would give me a menu and I would order idli, dosa, sambar. Wherever I went I would not stay in someone's house. I

would say, "Make arrangements in a hotel. I will not come alone and I will not come in less than first class." For just one lecture they would give hundreds of thousands of rupees because the subject that I had to teach was worth that. The knowledge that God gave me, nobody has. So I received a lot of help from these people.

The churches has also helped a lot. All the priests and churches are very affectionate, so affectionate that the priests had their heads shaved. I have this disease or this knack of getting people to shave their heads, wear geru and change their names. I give a name which is the name of God, and God has many names. "God, you have thousands of names. What name should I have written on your invitation?" If God is to be invited, what name should be written because He has thousands of names. So I give the same name to you and to Him. This is my disease.

Material wealth and spiritual wealth

In many European countries yoga has been given a special status by the government. The government gives aid and provides information about the best places to learn yoga. In Germany, those who learn yoga and take out insurance get a premium subsidized by the government. This happened in many countries after I had taught there. I did not only teach yoga. I used a little brain power also. I said, "A system should be made for teaching yoga in European countries." They have money, that is the reality. This is also important because of the lack of money in India. Here people are always worried about money, but this will not continue for long. Drinking too much milk or wine leads to vomiting and smoking more bidis causes coughing. As much as we take in, the same comes out. The cry of money will not work for very long because disinterest will develop after a while.

If you go on eating sweet things like halwa and kheer you will get diabetes. You want them one day, but not every day. In this way disinterest develops towards property and enjoyment. At your present stage you do not understand this. May God give you all the things that they have in western countries and then you will know why there is discontent there. What is the comfort in sleeping on the floor or the discomfort in sleeping on a mattress? You cannot know now because our ancestors have seen a lot of poverty. So may God give you things for your material prosperity. I don't need them.

The day before yesterday a man from overseas was sitting over there and a boy stole his camera and snatched his bag. The police weren't informed. The man said, "I don't care." Could any one of you local people say that? Think honestly. No one could say it because we are not in that circle yet. We are in the vicious ring of materialism, but it won't work for long.

Golden India

This will not continue in India for long. One day there will be prosperity in India, and on that day the knowledge that our ancestors have given in the Vedas will return. Because India was a golden bird, wasn't it? During the time of Lord Buddha, thousands of boys and girls had their heads shaved and took sannyasa. Today they can't do that because their father will say, "If you become a monk, who is going to feed me, who will earn in our home?"

How much prosperity there must have been in this country during the time of Lord Buddha! The period in which the knowledge of the Upanishads and Vedanta came, when people were doing yajnas in villages, that was the peak of prosperity. When there is excess, when man enjoys too much, then his mind moves away from enjoyment. This is natural.

It will happen again in India and at that time there will be no need for us to propagate yoga. We will not go to your door, but you will come to ours and ask where the guru lives. You will say, as many of you do say, "Guruji, we want to learn tantra." "We want to learn asana." "We want to learn the Yajur Veda." "We want to do yajna. We have

124

twenty lakh rupees." This period is going to come in this country.

India, a haven for the world

There is one more point. India, not now but in the near future, will become a place of shelter and security for America and Europe. That time is coming. This is a prophecy. Why? Because this is the only country which has a brain. No one country can establish its supremacy over the world for an endless time. For thousands of years India had its day, then it collapsed. Now America is also having its own day and it will collapse. Europe also had her own days and they will also end. But the greatest thing, the main thing, is that thousands of boys and girls are coming to the ashrams here from north and south.

Thousands of people are coming as the markets are opened in the field of business. This is a sign. Right now a global market is being opened in India. When it is completely open all these boys and girls will come here and they are very brilliant. Boys and girls aged twelve to fifteen can all start working here. They can do everything from computers to sweeping and cleaning toilets. They have training and they feel very good here. They can live without shoes and shirts, they can sleep on the floor. Their children can live without panties. A French woman is here and her child doesn't wear panties or use the toilet, he goes to the open fields. Their culture and mentality is changing. We want toilets, but they don't.

* * *

Sannyasa and the gurus

When the generator is not working who will connect the electricity? So long as the generator does not supply electricity, then who will connect us? There are five gurus and sannyasa is given in front of the five of them. The mantra guru cuts off the tuft of hair left at the back of the head, another gives the robes and the one who gives

125

knowledge is the *vidya guru*. Gurus are of many kinds and have different roles. Dattatreya had twenty-four gurus. Whenever you learn from someone, he is a guru. This is one simple definition.

Sannyasa and philosophy

Near my guru's ashram in Rishikesh, I learnt the teachings of the Upanishads in Raghavacharya's school of philosophy. He belongs to the line of Ramanujacharya, not that of Shankaracharya. The teacher used to say to me, "You are not God, you are a part of God." But in the books of Shankaracharya it is written, "You are God" – *Tat Twam Asi*. So I would have arguments with Raghavacharyaji every day, and I stopped going there. There were great arguments and fights.

Thereafter I went to Kailash Ashram. In those days Swami Vishnudevanandaji was the mahamandaleshwar. There we read *Panchadashi*, *Viveka Chudamani*, *Aparok-shanubhuti*, so I have learnt Sanskrit before. When sannyasa is taken rituals are performed. The brahmins are not called, but we have to perform the final rites of our father, grand-father and great-grandfather and thereafter we have to perform our own funeral rites, because according to sana-tana dharma, sannyasa is, in a way, civil death.

Sannyasa as a new birth

In a way it is a death according to the law. Our property law does not recognize this truth, and if I want to file a case against my brother about my ancestral property, then the law will recognize my claim. Still the scriptures do not support this. After sannyasa diksha you do not have a claim over your inheritance because you are dead and have achieved a state of civil death. The name changes, the gotra or lineage changes, and after sannyasa, caste and creed is not accepted. A sannyasin does not accept caste and creed. We know that for social reasons we are brahmins, kshatriyas, vaishyas, shudras, this or that, but that is in relation to a social system. God did not make a shudra a

126

shudra, or a brahmin a brahmin with special privileges; this we do not accept.

The next point is that after sannyasa one has no connection to the family because that was your past life. Sannyasa is called a new birth. The one who performs karmakanda, ritual, contributes what we call *pinda daan*. So we have completed our obligations. I have done the pinda daan of the person who was born in Almora or Kumaon, that one who died, and am free of that.

Mantra of sannyasa

Then there is a mantra which the guru gives. In Christianity there is the same system. The disciple is put into the water and then baptized. In our system also one has to descend into water and mantras are chanted, which are called *preshya mantras*. When you take sannyasa then we will tell you what they are, not now. They are divine mantras. They say, "I forsake heaven, I forsake earth, I forsake my own self, I leave everything. I have no connection with anyone. Let things come, let things go. If happiness comes, it is fine. If sorrow comes, it is fine. I am the witness of everything." It is said that light is the witness of everything and is similarly unaffected.

Organization of sannyasa

In Hardwar when the Kumbha Mela takes place, there are elections in the Niranjani Peeth. One is for the acharya, the other is for the store keeper, *kothari,* and the third is for the treasurer, *bhandori.* The Kumbha Mela is now taking place so another election will be held. The one who is elected is traditionally a good person, a simple person, and has no ego. Being a prominent person is nothing. In sannyasa the only basis for re-election is that one is a sadhu, pious. It is not necessary for one to be a prominent person. Maybe one commands great respect in society. "Look, he is a prominent person, he has a lot of money." In our system that is immaterial. But whether one is a sadhu or not is important. *Sadhu* means that one is a gentleman.

127

Dattatreya

Dattatreya's father was a great debauchee, a person of loose character. Yet his mother was devoted to her husband in accordance with *pativratte,* which is the principal duty of a women in our scriptures. Not only in our system, even in Christianity this is believed, and they provide a similar vow for men also. Although in their society it is not applicable, in their religion they believe in this. So Dattatreya's mother was named Anasuiya and his father was named Atri.

Atri used to go to a prostitute every day. Later his legs became weak and because of his condition, Anasuiya would support him on her shoulders when he went to the prostitute's house. Has any woman so much strength that she not only pardons her husband, but also accepts him? That calls for great courage and great power. That is a lofty personality. I am not saying whether it is good or bad, that is a separate point. I am talking about Anasuiya because her son, from the time of his birth, had the inherent traits of sannyasa. He used to say, "What is the use of wearing clothes? My mother did not give me clothes before birth."

Dattatreya is called the incarnation of *Trimurti,* the three faced one, meaning Brahma, Vishnu and Mahesh. He was born long ago. While walking the streets he would initiate anyone, even a cobbler or a sweeper, into sannyasa. The person would say, "O Lord, I surrender to thee," and Dattatreya would say, "Shave your head, apply ashes and keep only a yogadanda and a kamandala with you. Leave everything else. Eat only two rotis and lie down anywhere to sleep. If you die it is fine; if you are alive, it is fine."

He did not consider caste, creed or sect. Where he found a thirst for knowledge he authorized it, even for one born in a low caste family. His attitude was, "If you have a thirst for knowledge, then you have the right. We do not say that you should be born a brahmin or that you should be born in a well-to-do family. Knowledge is for everyone."

There are many stories about Dattatreya. Once he was passing a house where a woman was pounding rice husks and her bangles were making a noise. The mother-in-law

128

had a fever and told her daughter-in-law to stop, so she did. Dattatreya commented that when there is external noise, peace is disturbed, but the noise of the mind should also be stopped. In the same way he learnt something from an eagle, from a prostitute, from a monkey – he learnt from everyone. So they all became his vidya gurus, ones who give knowledge.

Dattatreya's mother was his diksha guru, the one who initiated him into mantra. The interaction of a pious mother and a debauched father gave a son born to be an *avadhoota*, a free sannyasin without any attachments, who doesn't even wear clothes. An avadhoota sees the world in a particular way and Dattatreya saw the world in a particular way.

* * *

Buy food not missiles

I have been everywhere, including Southeast Asia, Afghanistan and South America, but the poverty in India is of a different type. Governments in every country spend a lot of money on weapons and armour. They have missiles, fighter planes, every type of armoury and weaponry for fighting a war. The developed countries manufacture these war items, then the money of the undeveloped countries goes to them. Those who deal with fighter planes, missile technology and so on are very rich, fabulously rich. You are such prominent people, but if you have to go to London once or twice you will be thinking about how to get a free ticket. But an engineer can come here from London every year to visit his wife and travel all over India. They can afford this because they manufacture all the items of war and sell the technology at a very high price.

But the point is that whatever money is generated is not distributed amongst us. This is the doctrine of our economics. If in our country or any other country all the revenue which is generated by food grain production, export or other means was not spent on war items, then everyone would become happy. The whole of Africa is living

129

upon relief sent by the United Nations; you must have read about it in the newspaper. Things are sent by air: tents, houses, food, even water, clothes and security. What use is their own government? I do not understand a government which cannot run a country. When people are dying of hunger, what use is that government?

The duty of governments

The role of a government is to look after people. In the scheme of any country their role is supposed to be that of guardians. Take the example of North Korea. It produces many missiles, saying it will attack America! North Korea is a small nation. Children are dying from hunger there. For seven or eight years there has been no rain, the land is cracked and dry. What need is there for armour and weapons? They fear South Korea may attack. Even if it does attack what will happen? Ten or twenty thousand people will die. At the moment hundreds of thousands of children are dying there. Generations are being wiped out; all the children between two and six years old will die. Infants do not even need clothes, they only need nutrition, food. Now they do not get it. We have no solution to poverty. Whatever we do, whatever institutions do, is insignificant. It is like a cumin seed in a camel's mouth. Poverty will not be eliminated as long as the government does not behave like a parent. The relationship between a government and its subjects should be like that of a father and son. This has been the traditional view of our Indian culture – government as parents.

International poverty

We often used to go to South America, to Colombia, Argentina, Uruguay, and in the villages there we witnessed great poverty. Some nations in the world are so wealthy that it is really difficult to explain their wealth; they are really unbelievably wealthy. There are also nations where the per capita income is only forty to a hundred and fifty rupees a month. It is difficult for us to bridge this gap. For this a radical change is required in economic philosophy and in political philosophy. We do not think that democracy is a solution. We do not think it provides a way out. The basic structure of political philosophy should change.

Any king who rules should hold himself responsible for any mistake and there should be punishment for it too. That power of punishment is not with the subjects now and so there is no way to redress wrongs. One day Swami Satsangi went to the home of the pradhan of the village and found there was not even a grain of rice in his kitchen. And he is the chief of the village! He owns at least twenty or thirty acres of land. What will someone do with only fifteen acres of land? No one has access to an infrastructure. There are no oxen and a tractor is out of the question. There is seed, insecticides, pesticides and knowledge, and these farmers somehow make both ends meet with what they produce. I am not an anti-establishment person. It is not my nature to say anything about the establishment, but whenever I think of this, I feel sad and I know also that I have no solution. I know also that no one has the solution for this situation. Poverty seems to be an inevitable part of their destiny, as if it has the stamp of destiny from above.

* * *

Devotion and lifestyle

When you do not want to marry, then why live at home? You live in the house when you marry because then you have to live in a social system. When one doesn't want to marry, when one doesn't want to live with anybody, when one doesn't want progeny, one should live in seclusion. This actually is the truth. In order to convert emotion into devotion only intellectual effort is not enough; one has to change the situation also.

When we do not adopt the life of a householder, then it means that we do not really need the life of a householder. We do not need it, nor do we desire it. In such a situation we should find a place of seclusion and the best plan is to go to an ashram where we can transmute our feelings and emotions into devotion.

Devotion and guru

To convert the feeling of emotion into devotion, first of all a mould is needed, and the mould is the guru. One should have an emotional connection of bhakti with the guru. When there is rapport between guru and disciple, mental affinity, thereafter bhakti or devotion deepens. Devotion towards guru is, in reality, devotion towards God. All the scriptures, Upanishads and great men have said this.

All the scriptures, many saints and even Kabir say that the most difficult thing is to select a guru. The guru is also a human being made from the five elements just as your body is made from the five elements. As you live and are bound by the *gunas*, the three aspects of creation, so is the guru. In the most natural way he cannot be perfect, that is the first thing the disciple has to understand. If the disciple feels that at all times he wants to see total perfection in the guru, if he wants to see him without any blemishes, then this is not possible. Why speak of the guru? Such a disciple will see faults in Krishna and Rama.

Kajal kee kothari men kaisohun sayano jaaye
Eka daag uaahu ko laagihain pai bhagi hain.

Whoever goes inside a coal mine
Is more than certain to find a black mark here or there.

Guru and perfectionism

One should always keep one point in mind when searching for a guru. Remember that every human being is a perfectionist by nature. By perfectionist, I mean that every human being has some ideals and he wants to see those ideals. You want to see your own image. You have an ideal, and you want to see the image of it in me. The complex feeling or the mental block of your image of perfection is that you don't see what you want to see in me. I can never be it one hundred percent because you have created a sense of perfection from some complex or some mental block. You have created a psychological barrier in yourself. This needs to be understood. In the science of human psychology, perfectionism is a complex. It is your personality barrier.

Every person has a preference and he watches to see whether or not he can get that preference. While going to a shop to purchase a sari, you look to see whether the shopkeeper is a brahmin or not. Why are you concerned with that? You have to purchase a sari. You want to purchase a good sari, but for you the shopkeeper should be an old man and a brahmin, and he should be neither too tall nor too short. We call this perfectionism.

Clean your mirror

A perfectionist prepares a barrier in the mind and that barrier is created for his security, because basically everybody is insecure. A human being has four instincts: food, sleep, sex and fear. The meaning of fear is insecurity; it is ingrained in everyone. Therefore, one has to be aware of this while searching for a guru.

When I went to Rishikesh looking for a guru I went to Kailash Ashram first. I asked Swami Vishnudevananda for sannyasa, but he said, "When you take sannyasa I will be present, but go to Swami Sivananda. He is a sadhu and an educated person and you are also educated."

So I went to Swami Sivananda and said, "I have come here to live with you." He said, "Okay, live here but first of all clean your mirror. Whatever you want to achieve is within you, it is not within me. The guru doesn't give anything. The soul, the atma, is the truth within us. Consciousness is within us, the light is within us. Brahma is within us. Everything is within us."

> *Yaa ghat bhitar saat samandar*
> *Yaa ghat bhitar nau lakh moti*
> *Yaa ghat bhitar sarjanahara*
> *Avadhu andhadhundh andhiyara.*

133

There are seven oceans inside this body
There are nine lakh pearls inside this body
There is the Creator inside this body.
Oh Avadhoota! There is darkness all around.

Beyond darkness is a light that is within us. You must see that you are tied to the guru, that's all.

Now, maybe that guru drinks tea, two, three or four times a day and wears leather shoes, or sleeps and snores during the day. Why do you see all this? When the heart accepts, the brain does not play any role. When you love, the brain should not be allowed to come in between, otherwise it will spoil the whole thing. Therefore, to transform emotions into bhakti, establish your relationship with the guru.

Guru seva

Service to the guru is of many kinds. Lord Krishna used to collect wood at Sandipani's place. Do you now where Lord Rama used to live at Vashishtha's place? Rama who was the prince of Ayodhya? In Vashishtha's cave, where Vashishtha himself used to live, ninety-six miles away from Rishikesh, near Brahmapuri, right on the bank of the river Ganga. Shatrughana used to live next to Swami Sivananda's ashram and Bharat used to live in Rishikesh proper. Lakshman used to live where Lakshman's bridge is now.

The four brothers were living at four different places and Vashishtha was living ninety-six miles away. If you see that area now in this Computer Age, it is forest and mountain, and then, in Treta Yuga, God knows how many lions and leopards must have been roaming about. Still, life is spent like this with the guru.

Lord Rama spent his life with his guru. He worked with a spade, looked after the cows and buffaloes, picked up wood for the ashram. Maybe he also washed Arundhati's clothes. Who knows? He must have done everything as service. He must have travelled back and forth daily, and it would not have been on horseback. While living in the

134

gurukul, he had to follow the rules of the ashram. He had to sleep on the floor, which was the rule in the ancient period. Lord Rama had to lead a hard life and he was trained in his guru's ashram. As it is said,

Guru griha gaye padhan Raghurai
Alpa kaal vidya sab paayee.

Rama went to his guru's place to study.
In a very short time he received all knowledge.

He from whose mouth the Vedas and shrutis emerge, also comes to this world to study for lila.

Later on, when Lord Rama was exiled to the forests, he did not feel the pain and hardship of forest life because the austerity of his guru's ashram had made the pain of life lighter. The austerity of the guru's ashram renders that service. The difficulties which come in life are of many kinds. They are in the form of pain: poverty is pain, hunger is pain, thirst is pain, disease is pain, criticism and back biting are pain; there are many types of pain. So these become lighter, insignificant.

The power of devotion

To turn emotion into devotion is not a joke. Mirabai's emotions changed into devotion because she was very innocent. She did not use her intellect, only her emotions. Had she used her intellect, she would have said, "How can wood be my husband?" But from childhood, when she was given a wooden idol of Krishna, she accepted it as her husband. The meaning of husband is husband. The one whom one marries is called husband, the one with whom a woman lives for her whole life is called husband. She changed her emotion to devotion and she was successful. When emotion is changed to devotion, it becomes very powerful. It can overcome a cup of poison sent by the king.

That wonder happened in her life and the same thing happened with Chaitanya Mahaprabhu. He was an intellectual, a professor of law. He was a preceptor and had

135

completed his doctorate, a thesis on logic, which is called a PhD these days. Although he was a great intellectual, he kept his intellect aside and established a connection with God. The connection that Chaitanya Mahaprabhu established with Krishna cannot be understood by the brain; it is so simple.

Neither the emotion of Mirabai nor of Chaitanya Mahaprabhu can be understood. Even the sentiments of Ramakrishna Paramahamsa towards Kali are not the subject of intellect. Therefore, to convert sentiments into devotion, first let the intellect retire – suspend it, dismiss it. Sri Aurobindo has clearly written, "Intellect is the barrier and reason is the barrier." In spiritual life, reasoning, arguments and intellect do not work. Why don't they work? Because the search you are making is for something not seen by anyone.

You have not seen it, you don't have proof. You don't have a chart saying, "Go this way." There is no timetable, no way is known. Is God a woman or a man? Is God a man or an animal? Is God there or not? If it is void, what is void? If it is *nirguna*, without any qualities, what does that mean? God is not the subject of argument, God is not the subject of intellect. God is the subject of emotion and that emotion which changes into devotion. Highest love is the form of devotion. Devotion, bhakti, is not love, it is highest love. After drinking that and making others drink it, you are intoxicated, intoxicated, intoxicated. They are three, not one. Highly intoxicated means drunk, passed out. After drinking wine this happens. In the third stage there is no awareness of the world. It is not such an easy path.

Pravritti and nivritti
When you don't have to lead the life of a householder then why live in a household? I can't understand that. If you have to be a householder, if you have to get married, have children, this and that, then that is a different path. Live it. That is also a way. There are two conditions: *pravritti*, attachment to worldly objects, and *nivritti*, accomplishment without self-interest. The *Gita* (3:3) says this clearly :

Loke'smindvividhaa nishthaa puraa proktaa mayaanagha
Jnaanayogena saankhyaanaam karmayogena yoginaam.

"In this world there is a twofold path, as I said before, O Sinless one; the path of knowledge of the Samkhyans and the path of action of the Yogins."

When I don't have to get married and stay at home, when I don't have to do anything, don't have to earn my way, then why should I live the pravritti path? I should follow the nivritti path. And even if I do live the pravritti path for many years, this pravritti can be a kind of nivritti because accomplishments without any attachment do not affect life. There are no seeds, no karmas are formed, and the sentiments gradually go through metamorphosis by themselves. There is transformation of sentiments.

This is a very lengthy subject. In our scriptures, the bhakti path is dealt with and in the end we define sentiments as bhavana, feeling. How will you define feeling? What is the meaning of feeling? What is the meaning of heart? I am answering you directly and all those who are in your position. When the feeling of detachment arises in the mind, at that moment a person should renounce the world, otherwise the mind will change.

This detachment is a great thing. Say you are a girl. In our society girls are still insecure. Therefore, after seeing what a good environment it is, you should go and live in an ashram. In India there are many good ashrams. But in an ashram a disciple need not do pooja and ceremonial worship. Only service is necessary.

Serve day and night so that the mind is neither here nor there but remains hanging in between. For example, where is Swami Niranjan's mind? That innocent fellow's mind remains hanging in the middle. He can never get a foothold in his mind. As soon as he finds his feet, he gets another duty. With me it was the same. For so many years I did not even know that I had a mind. Therefore, in the ashram seva, service, meaning physical work or even the smallest service, will give you a great boon.

137

Mosquitoes

When I went to Rishikesh to live with my guru, he had nowhere for me to live. There was a ruined inn nearby and I lived in one of its rooms. If you could have seen it – on this side scorpions, that side mosquitoes! I was so afraid of mosquitoes. Even today I am afraid of mosquitoes, but I am not afraid of snakes. You can put snakes around my neck and still I will coolly give a lecture. I have made this area mosquito free. We look after the ground. Wherever there is a hole, I have it filled it so there will be no mosquitoes.

Swami Niranjan: Swamiji, if mosquitoes are so dangerous then why do they exist?

Sri Swamiji: Maybe nature has created mosquitoes for genetic transfer. What other creature in the world can transplant genes from one creature to another? Maybe the variety of creatures that you see in the world, eighty-four lakh *yonis* they are called, are all due to the grace of mosquitoes. That creature is bitten by the mosquito and then it comes over and bites these creatures and transfers the genes here. Then after this, the offspring of that generation will have different, changed qualities; even its method of thinking will change.

Is it only the mosquito, only this one creature? A fly does not do this. In the botanical world the butterfly and honey bee do some kind of genetic transfer from here to there and from there to here. You all know that. You have studied it at school. Mosquitoes have a very great role to play and not only here in India. If mosquitoes died through-out the world, then propagation would stop. Then there would be no creature which could bite you and then infect another person, or bite me and then infect you! No other creature can do that, only the mosquito.

I have thought about this. After all, why has God created mosquitoes? In nature, whatever is created is created for some purpose. There is nothing in this world without pur-pose. What could be the purpose of the mosquito? To spread malaria and filaria? No. Then slowly, one day in a deep state of meditation I felt that a mosquito bit a dinosaur

138

and transplanted its genes into a fish. After a few generations those fish started moving towards land and became lizards. It happens after ten thousand years, after twenty or thirty thousand years. Genetic transfer does takes place; it comes in the DNA factor. It is a reality. Because of this there are differences in human beings. Tell me, in the world, amongst six billion people, have you seen two people with the same face? Do they have the same fingerprints? No, they are all different.

Genetic disease

There are many diseases also due to this genetic transfer. Among them diabetes is important. There is a diabetes which is genetic. You will not be able to cure it, even with yoga. Although many people's diabetes is cured, many do not get cured even by yoga. Genetic diseases will not be cured. Although I have cured thousands of people of arthritis, thousands were not cured. If the base is genetic, it will not be cured. If it is just due to cold or heat, or due to calcium and calcification, that type is curable. There are many genetic diseases which cripple the body. Some deformities are genetic and diseases like cancer are basically genetic. In Europe there is so much cancer. I have seen so many people die young. I thought maybe it happened because their genetic transfer does not take place according to scientific technique.

I am referring to sexual transfer. The offspring born out of just any union between a girl and a boy is not called proper progeny. The right progeny is obtained through proper genetic transfer. Therefore, in our Hindu religious scriptures, although people say they are very out of date, there is a proper foundation for the system of lineage, the descending and ascending system. The system of race and caste is the foundation of this. The basis of caste is not untouchability, or a distinction between high and low. Caste identifies a genetic group.

You are educated people, you can understand this. Caste represents a genetic group. Clan or *jaati* does not

139

mean caste. In English we say caste, but really jaati is derived from the Sanskrit word *gyati,* meaning identity. The word that you should use is identity, not caste. Then varna means we get to know that you belong to the red, yellow or white category. The identification of a person or jaati gives the basis of identity, the genetic group. Marriage should never take place within one genetic group. It will lead to destruction, more diseases and more fighting.

* * *

Rishikesh

Swami Sivananda was a great devotee from South India and he wanted to build a temple to Lord Vishwanath in Rishikesh. Now from where were we to bring water? A lot of water is needed for construction and the Ganga is a long way down from the ashram. Those who have been to Rishikesh know that. In those days there was no electricity in Rishikesh and no generator. I saw electricity and generators for the first time only in 1950. Anyway we went up to Tapovan village where there was a waterfall, cut a drain in the hill over a period of fifteen days and built a big water tank, forty by twelve feet.

I was so thin and lean that people used to tease me. People coming from outside would say, what type of brahmachari is he? My cheeks were dry and sunken and you could count every bone on my body. I was so lean and thin that there was no charm in my face. I had no fat on my body or muscles but so much energy that I could cross the Ganga five times a day. If you asked me to climb a tree I would climb like a monkey. So it was my duty to fill up the water tanks in the ashram from the Ganga, fifty buckets daily. Bringing bel leaves from the forest for the worship of Lord Shiva was also one of my duties.

All knowledge is within you

Sometimes I was asked to clean the library and while dusting I would see the Rig Veda, the Yajur Veda and the Sama

140

Veda there. This was a great temptation. The Upanishads and other texts used to tempt me.

I said to Swamiji, "There are so many books. Can I take a few?" He replied, "Satyananda, you are talking of infection, you should talk of education. Infection is when knowledge comes in from outside. When inner knowledge is revealed outside, that is called education. All knowledge is within you. The knowledge of the four Vedas is within you. The human being is all knowledgeable. Atma, your spirit, is omniscient." He used to say that every creature, not only mankind but every creature, basically, fundamentally is God. There is that seed within it which is called atma and paramatma.

I am repeating the same thing in a different way. Knowledge is within us. What will you achieve by reading the Vedas? I kept working for twelve years and after that I was told to teach yoga. Believe it or not, I have never read a book on yoga. I have written them, but I have never read any books on yoga. I have just turned the pages of a few like the *Yajnavalkya Samhita*, *Gorakh Samhita*, *Gherand Samhita* and Swatmarama's *Hatha Yoga Pradipika*. I have seen them all, but I have not read any because I was convinced by Swami Sivananda that it is all within me.

December 1, 2000

Serve the guru

By serving the gru and serving him endlessly, the ego of the disciple is effaced. He does not think, "I came to the guru for self-realization and he is only getting me to do all the cleaning. He gets me to clean the toilets! In me he has an unpaid servant." The disciple should have faith in the guru. Always remember that all gurus are good. The guru who becomes a guru so he can cheat others cannot last long because he also has a soul.

Everybody has an inner conscience. A thief has a conscience, a dacoit has a conscience, a prostitute has a

141

conscience. One who becomes a guru to cheat others changes. Gurus do not cheat for long and nature punishes those who do. Many have been punished. So I am telling everybody that they should serve the guru.

There are many examples like Upamanyu, Uddalaka, Aruni, Rama and Krishna. Take the example of Swami Vivekananda. He belongs to our times, but there were no aeroplanes then and people used to travel only by ship. How much time did Swami Vivekananda get for his work? Twelve or fifteen years. In those few years what a strong foundation of Vedic dharma and knowledge of Adwaita Vedanta he laid in America. No one can forget it. Even today no church and no institution can break that foundation in the West.

How much time did Adi Shankaracharya get? He passed away after a lifespan of thirty-two years. During that period he triumphed in all directions from the north to the south of India and silenced Buddha Dharma, which had become the religion of the kings. In Badrinath the image of Narayana, which had had been thrown in the Alakananda river and replaced with a statue of Buddha, was reinstalled. What a powerful person he must have been.

He also came here to Baidyanath Dham. He wrote, "*Poorvottar jvaalikaanidhane*," which means that amongst the twelve jyotirlingams this one is *poorvottar*, the north-easterly one. All the mountains around here are volcanic. *Jvalika* means volcano, so this must have been known as an extinct volcano two thousand years ago, when Shankaracharya made this reference. Today it is not a volcano. Today it is a mountain called Trikut.

* * *

God as Mother

God can very comfortably, very logically and also very scientifically be conceived of as Mother. It is much easier and much more natural to see God as Mother. I don't object to seeing God as Father. But for a child the relationship with the father is a distant one compared to the relationship with the mother. The relationship of a child with its mother is not only intimate but intense and very natural, because the child is nurtured by the warmth drawn from the mother and maintained by the mother's milk in every respect. If I begin to tell you about that, it will take hours, days, years and aeons to put it all before you. My point is that it is far easier, much more real, natural and practical to conceive of God as Mother. This is what we Indians, particularly the Hindus, believe.

Shakti worship

The worship of Mother is shakti worship. *Shakti* means energy, capacity, ability and potentiality. Indians who follow the rituals and traditions of the Vedas have conceived of God, have perceived God, have worshipped God and have believed in God in many, many forms. In the form of animals, in the form of divinities, in the form of human beings, in the form of air, water, fire, and so many other forms; forms and formless.

They say that if you have any difficulties in life, just forget everything and go to Mother. Go to your Mother. Go to your God, God as Mother. Mother will never consider your sins. A child may become a bad child, but Mother never becomes a bad Mother. Mother is always kind and Mother is always compassionate, She does not punish Her children. She may give them a slap sometimes but it is out of love, not anger. Mother is not jealous of Her children. My Mother, my God, is not a jealous God.

My Mother is such a beautiful lady and She uses beautiful ornaments. Her nose is beautiful, Her forehead is beautiful, Her cheeks are beautiful, Her lips are beautiful, Her breasts are beautiful, Her plait of hair is beautiful, Her eyes are beautiful, Her ears are beautiful, Her ornaments are beautiful, Her waist is beautiful, Her hips are beautiful. She is nothing but beauty, nothing but grace, nothing but kindness. Never will She frown on you, but She will destroy all the evil qualities in you – the *rakshasas*, the demons, the

143

black forces, the dark forces. That is why She incarnates in us. May that Mother incarnate in you to destroy all the internal demons, so that you may then realize the grace of the divine.

Shakti worship is very ancient, much more ancient than Islam, Christianity, Judaism, Zoroastrianism, more ancient than Vedic religion. The first thing that man saw and began to worship, adore and revere was the Mother.

There was a time when a child did not know who his father was and did not care. Even today we do not care who the father is. Society wants to know because the law requires it, but apart from that you can say that father is a redundant principle in life. It is a fact! He did his job when he did his job and beyond that he has no role to play in your life. Only she has a role to play. These are very important things that modern people have to learn!

So shakti worship is a very ancient form of worship and its basis is tantra. Tantric worship is more ancient than Vedic worship. Tantric was the first, then Vedic, then Zoroastrianism and Judaism, then Christianity and then Islam. Slowly Mother was replaced by a very arrogant force called Father. He has no idea what a child needs. He thinks that a child only needs money and television.

Destroying the demon vasana
Today the Devi Pooja is going to be completed and we pray, "O Lord, keep everyone happy. Give discriminative wisdom to everyone and descend into everyone's heart so that all the demons, Mahishasura, Shumbha, Nishumbha, Chanda, Munda and Dhumralochana are destroyed." Then the mind becomes pure, the mental atmosphere becomes totally healthy, there is absolute bliss and all the demons in us are annihilated. By the Mother's grace the demons are totally eliminated. But the most difficult demon is Raktabija. If you slit his throat as many demons are created as there are drops of blood. So in his case Kali herself has to descend with a skull. You cut him, blood flows, she catches it in the skull and drinks it.

144

This Raktabija that resides in us is called *vasana*, or inherent desire. This vasana is such that it never ends. It remains even after you take sannyasa, even after renunciation, even after one renounces the loincloth. The vasana for women does not remain, nor for wealth, but one vasana does remain and that is for the body. The vasana for the body, "I exist," remains and there is no end to this. The only end to this vasana according to our saints and according to Vedanta lies in *jivanmukti*, liberation while in the body, with the grace of the goddess Mother.

Learn the Path

So all of you sit tight and remain in your places. Don't wander around looking for snacks. You won't die if you don't eat for a day, in fact you'll live one day longer by not eating for a day. When you go home you should make a sankalpa, "O Lord, may there be Sat Chandi Yajna every year in Rikhia and let us all go there, sit steadily and recite the mantras." This year two to four hundred people did the recitation. Not everyone could do it. So now everyone should learn how to recite the Sat Chandi Path from a teacher or pandit. If you make that sankalpa, then every year we will do Sat Chandi here. In our lifetimes we await such sacred and divine opportunities. That is my comment at the moment.

Although everyone contributed to the success of the yajna, two people stand out. One is Swami Satsangi. It is entirely her effort that has brought about the happy culmination of this event. When resolution is selfless that person's yajna is also successful and obstacle free. The second person is Srikant Goenka, who was your representative here and made the sankalpa on your behalf for your peace, plenty, prosperity and spiritual evolution. So I thank him on behalf of all of you.

Desire and sankalpa

When a person goes to a yajna, to the place of a deity or to a guru, then there is a desire in mind, a wish for something.

145

So have a desire, but also make a sankalpa. When you receive a big prize from God, when you get that lucrative job, do you offer only sweets worth two rupees? No, try to return what you received from God. Give something to God so that He says, "A son should be like that." You cannot deceive God. God is the cleverest in the world. He is called 'clever head'. Among clever people also there are the most clever. God knows all that you do and therefore He knows whatever sankalpa and whatever desire is in your mind. After all, when you are in the world there will be some desire, but you must promise something also in return.

Knowing what promise you have to make is difficult. But I made a promise. In December 1963 I went to Trayambakeswar. I said, "God, spread yoga throughout the whole world. My guru told me to spread yoga from door to door and from shore to shore, but nobody is ready to listen. One after another the people who used to invite me to do programs are becoming conspicuous by their absence." I said it in the same manner as I speak here. Then I said, "God, do something and when my work is completed I will leave everything to You. This I promise."

I worked, and in 1983 I saw that yoga classes had been started in all continents. Governments had accepted yoga and were providing assistance. Families had accepted yoga. Boys and girls, after shaving their heads, were coming to take up their stations. So I thought, "Sannyasi, the time has come. God, I surrender to You."

In 1988 I told Swami Niranjan that now he would have to manage the ashram and I went to Trayambakeshwar. In Trayambakeswar I said, "I have come. Now tell me what I have to do. I have no work. I have left Munger."

My Ishta said, "Go to Deoghar because from Deoghar you can get a ticket to go up." Deoghar is a cremation site of Sati, of Sashi Shankarji. I have applied for a ticket but I am still on the waiting list. I am not joking. I have come here to Rikhia for that.

Now I don't ask. I know. Why disturb Him again and again?

Gaalib na kar hajur men too arja baar baar
Jahir hai teraa haal sab un par kahe bagair.

Kabir says, "Do not tell God about yourself again and again. He knows all about you without being told."

Sankalpa to give

"God, give me enough so that I can give to others" – this should be your prayer. Do not pray only for your own television set and motor cycle. It is said that a boy went to the curd shop and asked for an earthen pot. The curd seller said, "An earthen pot is not available for free. Give me half a rupee." So the boy went to his father, who said, "Buy the curd for half a rupee and you will get the earthen pot free."

You are being given such a good opportunity to gain virtue. It is your good fortune that instead of giving only to your own you can give to so many. Hold fast to your faith in God.

Namo Narayana

Glossary

Aadesh – order, command, instruction

Aagama – tantric texts; scriptures piercing the depths of the soul; esoteric tradition of tantra

Abhishek – sacred rite including chanting of a Path dedicated to the deity and anointing the symbol

Agotra – not of the same genetic goup or family

Akhanda – unbroken, uninterrupted

Akhara – a training ground particularly for sannyasins

Alakh Bara – invisible boundary; a secluded place which preserves sannyasa traditions

Antaryamin – the inner ruler, God, ruler of the heart

Anushthana – resolve to perform mantra sadhana for a particular period of time with absolute discipline

Arati – ceremonial waving of lights

Archana – worship of an external form

Arjuna – the disciple of Sri Krishna in the Bhagavad Gita; one of the three son's of Kunti and the king Pandu

Arya Samaj – a reformist group founded by Swami Dayananda Saraswati, interested in re-establishing Vedic customs and upliftment of women

Asura – demon

Atharva Veda – last of the four Vedas to be composed

Atma – the self beyond mind and body, spirit, soul

Atmabhava – feeling yourself in others

Avadhoota – an enlightened saint perpetually in the state of transcendental meditation

148

Avidya – ignorance

Avyaya – non-decaying, imperishable

Baidyanath Dham – a temple of extraordinary power in Deogarh, dedicated to Lord Shiva

Bel patta – leaves of the sacred bel tree which is associated with Lord Shiva

Bhakti – complete devotion to a higher principle of life; love for all beings; devotion as service

Bhakti marga – the path of bhakti

Bhavana – feeling, emotion; ability to perceive subtle vibrations

Bhoga – experience of, and craving for, pleasure and enjoyment

Bhramaranada – a humming sound like a bee heard in one stage of meditation

Brahman – ultimate reality.

Brahmin – the priestly caste; one who is spiritually inclined

Chetan purusha – God, consciousness, total consciousness

Chitabhoomi – cremation ground

Crore – ten million

Daan – gift, philanthropy

Daan Yajna – donating something with devotion

Darbar – an assembly in the presence of a monarch or law giver where justice can be received, a place where everybody can be heard

Darshan – real vision; blessing received just by seeing an enlightened or divine being or God

Dasha indriyani – 'ten senses': hearing, touch, sight, taste, smell, vocal cords, hands, feet, genitals, anus

Deoghar – the burial ground of the consort of Shiva in her form as Sati; the main town in Rikhia, where Sri Swamiji presently resides; 'God's house'

Deva – a self-luminous being in a male form

Devata – illumined form, divinity that dispels the darkness and reveals the hidden essence.

Devi – a self-luminous being in a female form

Devotthan – awakening, arousing or invoking the divine force

149

Dharma – natural role we have to play in life; duty; righteous conduct

Dravidian – belonging to the original inhabitants of India

Durga – the goddess who defeated the demons when the gods were helpless; the divine mother; one of the manifestations of the consort of Shiva

Dwiragaman – farewell ceremony when a bride goes to live in her husband's house for the second and final time

Ganapati – another name of Lord Ganesha

Ganesha – elephant-headed, one-tusked deity; remover of obstacles; symbol of all that is auspicious, wealth, knowledge and attainment

Gotra – family name; one born in the same family or genetic group

Granth – a literary composition

Guna – quality: tamas, rajas and sattwa

Guru Granth Sahib – the sacred text of the Sikhs

Gyati – clan, genetic group or code; identity, see jaati

Hanuman – heroic devotee of Lord Rama who took birth as a monkey and aided in the rescue of Sita

Ikshwaku – the solar dynasty of Sri Rama

Ishta devata – personal deity

Ishwara – higher state of existence and consciousness

Itihasa – history, historical book

Jaati – clan, circumstances of life into which you were born

Jhulan – swing

Jivanmukta – a person who is liberated while alive

Jivatma – individual soul

Jnana – wisdom

Jnana shakti – the capacity to know

Jyotirlingam – self-existing, oval-shaped stone symbolizing Lord Shiva; there are twelve such lingams in India

Kali – powerful black goddess; the Mother capable of protection and destruction

Kali yuga – current era of the world, difficult and full of strife

Kalyanam – welfare, well-being

Kamandala – water pot

Kanya – virgin

Karka Sankranti – summer solstice, 16th July, when the sun enters the sign of Cancer

Karma – action and result; also implies devoted action to alleviate the suffering of the afflicted

Karmakanda – the part of the Vedas that relate to ceremonial acts and sacrificial rules; daily rituals of worship for a householder

Karna – the son of Kunti and the Sun god, famous for his courage in battle and his generosity of spirit

Karna Chaura – the fort of Karna; the hillock where Ganga Darshan is situated

Kartik – the lunar month of Kartik (October/November)

Krishna – incarnation of Lord Vishnu; the guru of Arjuna in the Bhagavad Gita, historical ruler of India, beloved of the gopis; 'dark'

Kulakund – pit from which the original kundalini shakti emerges

Kundalini – the divine energy that transforms human consciousness; evolutionary force

Kunti – a woman who called down the Sun god through the power of mantra and abandoned Karna, her son to him, in favour of marriage with King Pandu

Lakh – one hundred thousand

Lakshman – brother of Rama; a hero of the Ramayana

Lakshmi – consort of Lord Vishnu, goddess of prosperity

Lalita – the red goddess associated with Sri Yantra

Mahabharata – one of the great historical scriptures of India that chronicles the lives and spiritual development of humans, devas, demons, animals and other beings

Mahamandaleshwar – a highly respected teacher within the sannyasa tradition who guides a considerable range of people and activities

Makar Sankranti – the time when the sun begins its journey into the northern hemisphere for half a year; 13th to 15th of January; winter solstice

Mantra – a sound revealed to sages in deep meditation which liberates the mind from bondage when repeated

151

Marga Sheersha – ninth month of Hindu year, November/December

Maya – illusive power of creation

Mimamsa – one of the six classical Indian philosophies: Tantra, Vedanta, Vaisheshika, Mimamsa, Yoga and Samkhya

Moksha – liberation from the wheel of birth and death

Mukti – salvation, emancipation

Muni – a wise person who values silence

Nada Brahma – Supreme Being in the form of a sound

Namo Narayana – a salutation amongst sannyasins; 'Salutations to you who are a form of Lord Narayana'

Narayana – the divine, eternal, unchangeable Lord of creation who lives in water; another name for Lord Vishnu

Navadha bhakti – nine stages of bhakti

Neem – tree with very bitter leaves used for many medicinal purposes due to its cleansing action

Nigama – knowledge, the Vedas, ritual procedures

Nirakara – formless, unmanifest.

Nirguna – without qualities

Nirodha – complete cessation of the patterns of consciousness, when the mind is under control

Nivritti – without vrittis or mental modification; spiritual life

Paisa – coin of little value; one hundred paise make one rupee

Panchadasi – one of the most respected and basic texts of sannyasa for Adwaita Vedantins

Panchagni sadhana – meditation in the middle of four fires at each point of the compass, the fifth fire being the summer sun overhead; sadhana involving mastery of the five internal fires: ego, attachment, desire, anger and greed

Panchayat – village parliament

Pandavas – the five sons of Pandu who opposed the Kauravas during the war recounted in the Mahabharata and the Gita

Paramahamsa – 'supreme swan'; highest stage of spiritual life; a tradition of sannyasa

Paramartha chintan – thinking of the highest good

Paramatma – supreme or sublime self; atma of the entire universe, of the individual as well as the cosmos.

Path – any set of mantras to be chanted

Pativratte – a woman's vow to honour her husband

Pinda daan – offerings made to the ancestors

Poornahuti – the final rite in a fire ceremony or yajna where fruits etc. are offered to the flames and a wish is made

Pradakshina – walking ceremonially around a revered object

Pradhan – first, headman of a village or community

Prakriti – active principle of the manifest world.

Prasad – blessed object; grace, purity

Pravritti – with vrittis or mental modifications; material life; see nivritti

Preshya – mantras repeated when receiving traditional sannyasa initiation

Purusha – pure consciousness

Rajas – under the sway of dynamism and selfishness which leads to pain; one of the three gunas

Rakshasa – demon, negative or self defeating force

Rama – hero of the Ramayana, seventh incarnation of Vishnu, the embodiment of dharma

Ramacharitamanas – the story of Lord Rama as a poetic composition written by Goswami Tulsidas

Ramayana – an inspired book in verse describing the life of Rama; the historical version is written by Valmiki in Sanskrit, the devotional version by Tulsidas in a colloquial language, Avadhi

Ravana – a most powerful demon who threatened the whole earth, abducted Sita and was vanquished by Lord Rama

Rig Veda – the most ancient of the four Vedas comprised of mantras

Rishi – a Vedic seer

Sadhana – regular spiritual practice

Sadhu – a pious person, one who does spiritual practices

Sagotra – of the same genetic group

Sakhi – female friend or attendant of the devi

Sama Veda – the Veda which explains how to chant mantras

Samskara – unconscious memory, mental impression

Sanatana dharma – eternal dharma

Sankalpa – positive affirmation, resolve

Sankirtan – singing of God's name

Sannyasa – dedication; complete renunciation of the world, its possessions and attachments

Saraswati – goddess of wisdom and the arts; another name for sushumna nadi; an underground river in legend

Sattwa – a balanced state of light and knowledge, one of the three gunas

Shakti – energy, force, power, Mother, vital energy force, manifested consciousness, female principle

Shankaracharya – the great teacher who revitalized the Shaivite tradition and established the Adwaita Vedanta philosophy, author of many yogic and tantric texts

Shiva – Supreme Consciousness; auspiciousness, Lord of the yogis, male principle

Shreya – spiritual blessing, spiritual abundance, transcendental gain

Shruti – scriptures heard by saints in meditation

Siddhi – perfection; psychic power acquired as a result of yogic practice or divine dispensation or birth; power resulting in control over the physical elements

Sita – an incarnation of Shakti as the wife of Lord Rama, kundalini shakti, mother goddess, daughter of earth

Smritis – Vedic texts transmitted by memory.

Soma rasa – juice from the soma plant of legend which causes spiritual awakening and intoxication when used properly but should be withheld from unqualified people; divine nectar

Sri Yantra – the most respected yantra, symbol of the goddess

Srishti – created universe, creation

Tamas – the quality of inertia, darkness; dullness, ignorance; one of the three gunas

Tantra – ancient science of inducing spiritual experience, 'expansion and liberation'; esoteric technique leading

154

one from outside into one's own self; one of the six classical Indian philosophies

Tattwa – element, essence; the five elements are commonly listed as earth, water, fire, air and space or ether

Treta Yuga – the 'Third Age' in which Lord Rama incarnated; one of the four yugas

Trimurti – God as having three aspects: Brahma, Shiva and Mahesh

Tripura Saundari – another name for Lalita, the supreme goddess of Tantra

Tulsi – holy basil plant

Tulsidas – author of the Ramacharitamanasa

Turiya – superconsciousness; fourth state of consciousness

Unmani – a state where mind drops away, a transcendental state; 'no-mind'

Vashishtha – celebrated seer, family priest of the solar race of kings and author of several Vedic hymns

Vedanta – one of the six systems of Vedic philosophy; a philosophy based on the Vedas, 'end of perceivable knowledge'

Vedas – ancient spiritual scriptures: Rig Veda, Yajur Veda, Sama Veda and Atharva Veda

Vidya – knowledge, particularly of spiritual truth or reality

Vikshipta – oscillating state of mind

Vishnu – the aspect of the Supreme concerned with maintenance or preservation often associated with water

Vritti – mental modifications

Yajna – sacrificial rite, offering oblations to the fire

Yajur Veda – 'prose Veda'; explains the rituals in the Vedic ceremonies

Yoga – union; yoke; methods and practices leading to a conscious union of human consciousness with the divine principle; one of the six classical Indian philosophies

Yogi – one who has attained yoga

Yogini – female yogi

Index

157

INTERNATIONAL YOGA FELLOWSHIP MOVEMENT (IYFM)

The IYFM is a charitable and philosophical movement founded by Swami Satyananda at Rajnandgaon in 1956 to disseminate the yogic tradition throughout the world. It forms the medium to convey the teachings of Swami Satyananda through its affiliated centres around the world. Swami Niranjanananda is the first Paramacharya of the International Yoga Fellowship Movement.

The IYFM provides guidance, systematized yoga training programs and sets teaching standards for all the affiliated yoga teachers, centres and ashrams. A Yoga Charter to consolidate and unify the humanitarian efforts of all sannyasin disciples, yoga teachers, spiritual seekers and well-wishers was introduced during the World Yoga Convention in 1993. Affiliation to this Yoga Charter enables the person to become a messenger of goodwill and peace in the world, through active involvement in various far-reaching yoga-related projects.

BIHAR SCHOOL OF YOGA (BSY)

The Bihar School of Yoga is a charitable and educational institution founded by Swami Satyananda at Munger in 1963, with the aim of imparting yogic training to all nationalities and to provide a focal point for a mass return to the ancient science of yoga. The Chief Patron of Bihar School of Yoga is Swami Niranjanananda. The original school, Sivanandashram, is the centre for the Munger locality. Ganga Darshan, the new school established in 1981, is situated on a historic hill with panoramic views of the river Ganges.

Yoga Health Management, Teacher Training, Sadhana, Kriya Yoga and other specialized courses are held throughout the year. BSY is also renowned for its sannyasa training and the initiation of female and foreign sannyasins.

BSY provides trained sannyasins and teachers for conducting yoga conventions, seminars and lectures tours around the world. It also contains a comprehensive research library and scientific research centre.

SIVANANDA MATH (SM)

Sivananda Math is a social and charitable institution founded by Swami Satyananda at Munger in 1984, in memory of his guru, Swami Sivananda Saraswati of Rishikesh. The Head Office is now situated at Rikhia in Deoghar district, Bihar. Swami Niranjanananda is the Chief Patron.

Sivananda Math aims to facilitate the growth of the weaker and underprivileged sections of society, especially rural communities. Its activities include: distribution of free scholarships, clothing, farm animals and food, the digging of tube-wells and construction of houses for the needy, assistance to farmers in ploughing and watering their fields. The Rikhia complex also houses a satellite dish system for providing global information to the villagers.

A medical clinic has been established for the provision of medical treatment, advice and education. Veterinary services are also provided. All services are provided free and universally to everyone, regardless of caste and creed.

YOGA RESEARCH FOUNDATION (YRF)

The Yoga Research Foundation is a scientific, research-oriented institution founded by Swami Satyananda at Munger in 1984. Swami Niranjanananda is the Chief Patron of the foundation.

YRF aims to provide an accurate assessment of the practices of different branches of yoga within a scientific framework, and to establish yoga as an essential science for the development of mankind. At present the foundation is working on projects in the areas of fundamental research and clinical research. It is also studying the effects of yoga on proficiency improvement in various social projects, e.g. army, prisoners, children. These projects are being carried out in affiliated centres worldwide.

YRF's future plans include literary, scriptural, medical and scientific investigations into other little-known aspects of yoga for physical health, mental well-being and spiritual upliftment.

SRI PANCHDASHNAM PARAMAHAMSA
ALAKH BARA (PPAB)

Sri Panchdashnam Paramahamsa Alakh Bara was established in 1990 by Swami Satyananda at Rikhia, Deoghar, Bihar. It is a charitable, educational and non-profit making institution aiming to uphold and propagate the highest tradition of sannyasa, namely vairagya (dispassion), tyaga (renunciation) and tapasya (austerity). It propounds the tapovan style of living adopted by the rishis and munis of the vedic era and is intended only for sannyasins, renunciates, ascetics, tapasvis and paramahamsas. The Alakh Bara does not conduct any activities such as yoga teaching or preaching of any religion or religious concepts. The guidelines set down for the Alakh Bara are based on the classical vedic tradition of sadhana, tapasya and swadhyaya, or atma chintan.

Swami Satyananda, who resides permanently at the Alakh Bara, has performed the Panchagni Vidya and other vedic sadhanas, thus paving the way for future paramahamsas to uphold their tradition.

BIHAR YOGA BHARATI (BYB)

Bihar Yoga Bharati was founded by Swami Niranjanananda in 1994 as an educational and charitable institution for advanced studies in yogic sciences. It is the culmination of the vision of Swami Sivananda and Swami Satyananda. BYB is the world's first government accredited university wholly devoted to teaching yoga. A comprehensive yogic education is imparted with provision to grant higher degrees in yogic studies such as MA, MSc, MPhil, DLitt, and PhD to the students. It offers a complete scientific and yogic education according to the needs of today, through the faculties of Yoga Philosophy, Yoga Psychology, Applied Yogic Science and Yogic Ecology.

Residential courses of four months to two years are conducted in a gurukul environment, so that along with yoga education, the spirit of seva (selfless service), samarpan (dedication) and karuna (compassion) for humankind is also imbibed by the students.

YOGA PUBLICATIONS TRUST (YPT)

Yoga Publications Trust (YPT) was established by Swami Niranjan-ananda in 2000. It is an organization devoted to the dissemination and promotion of yogic and allied knowledge – psychology (ancient and modern), ecology, medicine, vedic, upanishadic, tantric darshanas, philosophies (Eastern and Western), mysticism and spirituality – nationally and internationally through the distribution of books, magazines, audio and video cassettes and multimedia.

YPT is primarily concerned with publishing textbooks in the areas of yoga philosophy, psychology and applied yogic science, research materials, practice texts and the inspiring talks of eminent spiritual personalities and authors aimed at the upliftment of humanity by means of the eternal yogic knowledge, lifestyle and practice.